Broadman Press / Nashville, Tennessee

D1475781

Sarah Walton Miller

BIBLE DRAMAS for OLDER BOYS & GIRLS

Dewey Decimal Classification Number: 812
Library of Congress Catalog Card Number: 75-95409
Printed in the United States of America
2.5My7118

CONTENTS

FOREWORD

This book contains ten plays based on the Scriptures. They are written for boys and girls in the eleven- to fourteen-year-old age range. Playing time varies from ten to twenty-five minutes. There are both differences and similarities in these plays. None are alike in method of presentation. All are alike in requiring a minimum of staging and props. All may be done in the sanctuary. Several have flexible casts.

These plays are intended as learning experiences. Simply to see a play is not enough. With each play is included a series of questions, a guide for discussion. Boys and girls learn while discussing what they have seen. The leader of such discussion needs to understand how to do this well, how to promote rather than terminate such valuable expression.

To the director, who may or may not have directed a play before, here are some explanations to help you. Stage left and right mean the actor's left and right. Upstage is back, downstage is front. A closed position means the actor moves away from the action and turns his own back toward the audience, indicating he is now out of the current action. In brief dramas with many exits and entrances, the closed position is usually preferable.

The word "freeze" used, herein, means the actor becomes motionless in a pose appropriate at that moment. He remains that way until his part calls for his entrance into the action. The expression "ad-lib" means the actors involved supply their own lines, appropriate to their characters in the given situation. Deciding on these lines can be a creative experience for the boys and girls.

In most of the plays, leaving all the lights on is in order. Any special lighting is listed in a particular play. If some of the boys and girls wish to create special lighting effects, let them. It need not be expensive. A slide projector makes a spotlight. Cans of various sizes, properly prepared, cost little and substitute for expensive equipment. (See "A Coin Is Missing" for instructions.)

In the majority of the plays biblical costumes are optional. (See pictures in elementary literature. Also see *Costuming the Biblical Play* by Lucy Barton.) Materials may be old dyed sheets, old bedspreads, or draperies. Use solid colors or stripes, not florals. The boys and girls are capable of designing their own costumes.

Scenery isn't necessary. Let the audience use the imagination God gave them. No painted piece is better.

To precede your play, why not use music? Or perhaps you might arrange the Scripture passage into a choral speaking piece for other boys and girls to recite.

1

The Man Who Built a Boat Anyway

If you haven't read the Foreword for helpful suggestions, do so now. Playing time is 17 to 20 minutes. Scripture basis begins with Genesis 6. Remember that the people around Noah worshiped Baal and not Jehovah. Look up Baal in a Bible encyclopedia. The Bible omits the name of Noah's wife and his sons' wives. Names are chosen for them. The people from the town may well have acted this way. They may have been even worse.

Costumes may be biblical or modern. Props needed are some small branches and a couple of chairs. The ark is apparently out of sight off to the right back.

Imagine the reaction to Noah's announcement. Think of your family trying to build a boat longer than a city block and as high as a three-story building. No wonder everyone thought Noah was crazy—in our play, at least.

CAST: NOAH *and his wife,* JERUSHA; *his sons and their wives:* SHEM *and* MILCAH, HAM *and* REBA, JAPHETH *and* TIMNA; *and the* TOWNSPEOPLE *1,2,3,4,5. These last may be boys and/or girls. Also, you may combine the parts for a smaller group of* TOWNS-PEOPLE, *or divide the lines among even more.*

> (*Lights off. When the lights come on,* NOAH *is kneeling center. The dots . . . show where* NOAH *listens to God, before he answers.*)

NOAH (*astonished*): . . . Water everywhere? Then we'll drown, Lord! . . . A boat? . . . (*agitated*) *That* big? Lord, we are farmers, not builders. No man ever saw a boat that big! . . . Yes, Lord, I hear you. . . . Very well, Lord, I will obey.

> (*Noah remains with head bowed for a moment, then rises and calls:*) Ham! Ham!

HAM (*off, calling*): Coming, Father! . . . (*enters right*) Yes, Father?

NOAH: Ham, go bring the family.

HAM: Everybody?

NOAH: Yes, hurry!

HAM (*surprised*): All right, Father.

> (*He leaves right. NOAH walks and thinks. Soon NOAH's wife, sons, and sons' wives enter right.*)

NOAH (*impatiently*): Sit down! Sit down!

> (*Some do and others stand behind those. All are puzzled.*)

NOAH (*continuing*): Listen, all of you. I bring strange news. Jehovah says—

JERUSHA (*aside to girls*): Oh, dear. Girls, there's trouble. He's been talking to Jehovah again.

NOAH: Jehovah says we must build a—a boat.

JAPHETH: Oh! Is that all?

SHEM: We don't need a boat. There's no water around here.

NOAH: Jehovah will send the water! Rains will come. Water will cover the whole earth. Jehovah has spoken!

REBA (*nervously*): Our farm?

NOAH: Everything. Land, buildings, even the highest mountains.

REBA: Oh, Ham, will we drown?

JERUSHA (*suddenly wailing*): Oh! Oh! My poor Noah! He's lost his mind! Oh! Oh! Oh!

JAPHETH: Father, you are frightening the women. You are joking?

NOAH: No, Japheth, I am not joking.

> (*Timna begins to cry*)

TIMNA: We'll all die.

JAPHETH: Stop crying, Timna. It is a mistake. Jehovah won't destroy the whole earth.

NOAH: Yes, he will.

HAM (*reasoning with his father*): Why would Jehovah destroy his world, Father?

NOAH: For the wickedness of men, that's why. Only we will escape. When we build that boat—the ark.

MILCAH (*her tender heart touched*): Everybody will—? Oh, the poor people. Even if they are wicked, still—(*She hides her face in her hands.*)

SHEM (*hand on her shoulder*): Don't cry, Milcah, don't cry. Father, look what you've done.

TIMNA (*tearfully*): Father Noah, is there no hope for the people?

NOAH: None, Timna. I grieve for them, too. But we must obey Jehovah. We will build the biggest boat ever built: 450 feet long, 75 feet wide, 75 feet high—three stories.

(*The women forget tears at this astounding project.*)

HAM (*excited*): Father, is this what Jehovah said?

SHEM (*protesting*): We can't build a boat that size!

JAPHETH: Think of the materials needed!

SHEM: Where will we find the plans?

HAM: Plans? How do you *begin* such a boat?

JAPHETH: Father, think of the space needed. From the house to the sheepcote, at least!

JERUSHA: Noah, listen to our sons. Surely your Jehovah did not say—

NOAH (*irritated*): Jerusha, why do you call him "my" Jehovah? You worship him, too.

JERUSHA: Then why doesn't he speak to one of us? You tell us he speaks to you. Why not to Ham or Japheth or Shem?

JAPHETH: Father, did you misunderstand this time?

HAM (*helpfully*): We can build a smaller boat, say 30 feet long.

NOAH: Ham, we need the ark for the animals.

MILCAH: What animals?

NOAH: Since everything on earth outside the ark will die, we must save two of every living thing, Milcah.

REBA (*shuddering*): Snakes, too?

NOAH: Yes, Reba. Snakes, too.

TIMNA (*astonished*): Now where will we get all those animals?

NOAH: We trust Jehovah to provide. We will gather them in and care for them until the waters go down again.

JERUSHA (*to the girls*): Girls, when Noah says *we* will care for something, he usually means *us*.

NOAH (*sternly*): Jerusha, you and the girls will do your share. Japheth, Shem, Ham, come! We will build the ark.

(*The men all leave right.*)

JERUSHA: Ark, indeed.

REBA: Mother Jerusha, do you really believe in Jehovah?

JERUSHA: I suppose. But I don't always believe in Noah. Don't ever tell, but Noah does get carried away sometime with his visions. I'll believe this flood when my feet get wet!

(*Lights off about five seconds. When they come on again, the women are downstage right tying twigs together for fuel. We watch them a few moments. Then we hear shouting off right. A group of agitated TOWNS-PEOPLE run on from upstage right and cross to downstage left.*)

TOWNS 1: Crazy men! Building that monstrosity on dry land!

TOWNS 2: Nasty old man! Yelling at us to "repent"! Repent what? What does he want us to repent?

TOWNS 3: Didn't you hear him? (*Mimicking*) "Flee the wrath of Jehovah or ye die!"

TOWNS 2 (*to 3*): He nearly caught up with you! (*Laughs heartily*)

TOWNS 4 (*to 3*): You *did* call him an old goat!

TOWNS 3: He *is* an old goat, the old goat. A *crazy* old goat!

TOWNS 5 (*dancing around mincingly*): Let's get even! Let's offer sacrifice to Baal to—to drop a tree on him! Or something like that.

TOWNS 3: His sons, too! Don't leave them out of the party.

TOWNS 5: Why not? A bargain: four get-evens for one sacrifice!

TOWNS 1 (*sees the women*): Look! There are their women. Let's have some fun!

TOWNS 2: Why not? We haven't done so well thus far.

TOWNS 1: Serve them right for living with those fools!

TOWNS 4: Come on! (*They approach the women who continue their work.*)

TOWNS 2 (*with a deep bow*): Greetings, fair ladies! You see before you pilgrims. Pilgrims to the shrine of a fool!

TOWNS 1: My friend means we came to see the talk of the country, that famous boat.

TOWNS 4 (*mockingly*): Ladies! When did you suspect your men were crazy?

JERUSHA (*losing her temper and running at* TOWNS 4 *with a stick*): Get out of here all of you!

TOWNS 4 (*eluding her*): Temper! Temper!

TOWNS 5 (*reaching out and pulling at her robe, then dodging when she tries to whack him*): Listen to our sweet hostess! Such a lady! Dear, dear, what a way to greet friends!

JERUSHA: You're no friends of ours!

TIMNA (*trying to calm* JERUSHA, *holding her back*): Jerusha, ignore them!

TOWNS 1 (*bowing to* TIMNA): Fair maid, you would ignore pilgrims? Pilgrims with such a great desire to see this wonder of the world?

MILCAH (*coming to other side of* JERUSHA): Go away!

TOWNS 5 (*to other* TOWNSPEOPLE): Don't forget, we are pilgrims come to "repent." Whatever that is!

> (*They laugh heartily, then begin to caper around all three women, chanting "Repent! Repent! We come to REPENT!" The women huddle together. Gradually the chant ceases and the* TOWNSPEOPLE, *tired of their game, and feeling once again resentful, stop before the women.*)

TOWNS 3 (*to* JERUSHA): Look here, woman. You look as if you have more sense than that old man of yours. Why is he building that thing?

TOWNS 4: We heard about it—that boat on dry land. So we came to see. We couldn't believe anyone would—

TOWNS 2 (*interrupting with a laugh at his own wit*): Now that we've seen it, we still don't believe it! (*All* TOWNSPEOPLE *laugh.*)

TOWNS 4 (*taunting*): Maybe you'll take us for a sail someday? Across the sheep pasture?

REBA: Why don't you just go away!

TIMNA: We aren't bothering you.

TOWNS 1: Listen to the girl. Friends, is she hinting that *we* are bothering *them*?

MILCAH (*pleading*): Please go!

TOWNS 5 (*mockingly*): My, my! How about a "pretty" please go? (*Turning angry*) You can't get rid of us that easy.

JERUSHA (*losing temper again*): Get out of here before I call Noah! . . . (*calling*) Noah! Shem! Ham! Japheth!

TOWNS 3 (*quickly*): We're going! We're going!

TOWNS 1: Yeah. Don't call that crazy old man again.

MILCAH: You are the crazy ones!

TOWNS 1: Do you see us building huge boats on dry land?

TIMNA: When the rains come and cover your city, you'll wish you had.

TOWNS 3 (*laughing*): Rains? Here? Listen to the woman!

TIMNA: The whole earth will be under water!

TOWNS 5 (*laughing*): That's enough! Come on, friends, let's go.

TOWNS 4: Wait! I want to give them all my blessing and say, "All of you deserve each other!" (*Laughs*)

TOWNS 2 (*bowing low*): Farewell, sweet ladies! We will all be back someday, to see that boat rot away! (*To* TOWNS-PEOPLE) That was a lovely rhyme, was it not?

(*The* TOWNSPEOPLE *leave left laughing. There is silence.*)

REBA (*after a pause, troubled*): Timna, do you believe the flood will come?

TIMNA: I don't know, Reba. But they made me mad!

JERUSHA: I always stand up for Noah, no matter what I think.

MILCAH (*remembering*): We all did, didn't we? (*They giggle*)

(*Noah and Shem enter right.*)

NOAH: What were you yelling for?

JERUSHA: We had—company.

NOAH: Those gabbling geese we chased off?

SHEM (*resentfully*): Hanging around, getting in the way, making fun.

NOAH: Forget them. Girls, go prepare packs for your husbands. They leave in the morning.

MILCAH: Where are you going, Shem?

SHEM: To gather up the animals. The ark is finished.

NOAH: While the men are gone, you women can begin loading in the stores. Go on, now.

(*The girls and Shem leave right.*)

JERUSHA (*pleading*): Noah, be more tactful with the townspeople. Please!

NOAH: Ignorant pagans! Worshipers of Baal!

JERUSHA: I don't care! It makes me mad when they call you crazy!

NOAH (*pats her shoulder comfortingly*): I know, Jerusha. Take heart. Remember, I do the will of Jehovah.

JERUSHA (*wistfully*): I hope so. Noah, are you *sure*? Only you ever hear him. All these months. That monstrous ark. Now the boys going off into who knows what dangers . . .

NOAH: No matter what happens, this is Jehovah's will.

JERUSHA: We obey *you*. If only we could believe, too.

NOAH: You can, Jerusha! Look up! See the clouds gathering?

JERUSHA (*looks up; turns away, disappointed*): They are only clouds, Noah.

(*Lights off five seconds. Remove all twigs. When lights come up, the sons are on stage, sitting, resting.*)

SHEM (*stretching*): Oh, it feels good to be home again! I am tired, tired.

JAPHETH: The best part of that job is—it's over.

HAM: Now what?

JAPHETH: Rest, I hope.

(*Their wives enter right.*)

TIMNA (*vexed*): You've been resting four days!

REBA: With those animals to look after, when do *we* rest?

HAM: Sit beside me, love. I'll hold your hand, and we'll rest together.

REBA: Don't try to change the subject. It is one thing to humor an old man.

MILCAH: Reba's right. It *is* one thing to go along as if it all made sense, but soon you will have to show Father Noah he is mistaken.

REBA: It would be kinder to tell him now.

HAM: Not yet.

REBA: We go on pretending to him that we believe?

HAM: We do. For now.

MILCAH: I don't know whether I can stand one more day of those animals! Either they go soon, or I do.

SHEM (*soothingly*): Now, Milcah—

MILCAH: All right, Shem, name the day!

HAM: Father says—

REBA: Don't put it all on your father, Ham. You all three went along with it all these months.

TIMNA: And made us follow!

REBA: First that ark. Now see what it's come to. All for an old man's dream, or whatever it was.

TIMNA: Japheth, admit it. You don't believe in that flood.

JAPHETH: Maybe.

TIMNA: Then go tell Father Noah right now. Turn all those animals loose.

JEPHETH: We'll wait.

MILCAH: Are you all *afraid* to tell your father he is mistaken? Afraid of an old, old man?

REBA: Think what you put him through. Those townspeople still come out here and jeer at him. Crazy Noah, they call him.

TIMNA: We all try to ignore them, but it is really awful. Please, Japheth.

JAPHETH (*sadly*): His faith in Jehovah is so—so strong.

MILCAH: What's the good of faith in a God who makes people despise you and call you names?

HAM: Wait a little longer, then we'll face him. Patience!

TIMNA: Patience? For nothing. All for nothing.

HAM (*sharply*): Stop complaining, all of you! Think of that old man. His terrible disappointment. He *believes*.

(*JERUSHA enters right.*)

JERUSHA: Hush! You are too loud! Your father will hear you.

(*NOAH enters right. All fall silent.*)

NOAH (*looking them over*): I did hear you.

Ham: Sorry, Father.

NOAH: Perhaps I am the one who should say that. You doubt. Shem? Japheth? All of you?

(*They look away, embarrassed.*)

NOAH (*continuing*): I didn't know. All this time. I believed, so I thought you believed, too.

JAPHETH: We are sorry, Father.

NOAH: I don't blame you. I remember you are young. I am old. I have followed Jehovah's will all my life.

MILCAH: Father Noah, we did not mean to hurt you.

REBA: You are good to us all.

JAPHETH: Now that it is out in the open, Father, the days are passing. Nothing happens.

NOAH (*sadly*): Are you all in such a hurry to see a world die?

>(*He walks apart, thinking. Soon Japheth follows.*)

JAPHETH (*gently*): Will you set a time limit, Father? A time we can set the animals free and take the ark apart?

HAM (*joining them*): The wood will bring something.

NOAH (*holds up a hand for silence*): Listen.

SHEM (*also joining them*): Please Father, you listen. Japheth is speaking for us all—

NOAH (*louder*): Listen, I say!

HAM: It's no use, Father—

NOAH (*shouting them all to silence*): Hush! LISTEN! All of you listen! Don't you hear? Don't you *hear*?

>(*All are motionless, listening, then looking up.*)

NOAH (*breaking the silence, speaks with great dignity*): Come. Let us go into the ark. It is beginning to—rain.

>(*We see them leave right, silent and awed. When they have gone, momentarily the lights are off, then on again in the audience.*)

Questions for Talking

1. Do you think it was hard for Noah to stand up against everybody?

2. Did it affect him as much as his family?

3. Did you ever stand against your friends for something you believed was right?

4. If you have the chance, will you have the courage to stand alone?

5. Do you understand the townspeople?

6. Did you like Noah's family? Why?

7. What does this play say to you?

2

Unwanted Brother

If you haven't read the Foreword for helpful suggestions, do so now. Playing time is 13 to 16 minutes. Scripture basis is Exodus 2. Look in a Bible encyclopedia under Aaron, Miriam, and Moses. Let someone report on Egypt's history between Joseph and Moses.

An added character to the story is the neighbor. She is imaginary but logical. The family had neighbors.

Biblical costumes may be worn or ordinary clothes with biblical headdresses. The ark may be a basket or box. A couple of chairs will suffice for staging.

CAST: AARON, *a boy about 12;* MIRIAM, *his sister, a year older;* JOCHEBED, *his mother;* AMRAM, *his father;* NEIGHBOR *woman.*

> (MIRIAM *enters right, speaking back off right to her mother.*)

MIRIAM: Rest, little Mother, rest. I will prepare the meal for Father and Aaron.

JOCHEBED (*calling from right, unseen*): Miriam! Do not let anyone know! . . . Miriam!

MIRIAM: I hear you. Do not worry. The Egyptian soldiers shall not find our new baby brother.

> (NEIGHBOR *woman calls from off left.*)

NEIGHBOR: Jochebed! Jochebed! Are you there?

MIRIAM (*anxiously running left*): Wait! I am coming!

> (*The* NEIGHBOR *enters before* MIRIAM *can stop her.*)

NEIGHBOR: Where is Jochebed?

MIRIAM: She—she is resting.

NEIGHBOR (*astonished*): Before the evening meal?

MIRIAM: She doesn't feel well. The heat of the sun yesterday.

NEIGHBOR (*suspiciously*): It is more than that, isn't it? She has borne a baby, hasn't she?

MIRIAM (*alarmed*): The heat of the sun makes many of us ill!

NEIGHBOR: I *knew* it would be soon! I told my husband last week I was sure. It's a *boy*, isn't it?

MIRIAM (*desperately*): What's a boy? You are imagining things.

NEIGHBOR (*loudly*): Oh, no, I'm not! You must report it. You must *report* it now!

MIRIAM: Report what? That the sun in Egypt is hot?

NEIGHBOR: The soldiers must come and take your *boy*!

(JOCHEBED *enters.*)

JOCHEBED (*worried*): Good day, neighbor! I heard your voice and came to welcome you.

NEIGHBOR (*still angry*): Now will *you* deny it, too?

JOCHEBED: Deny what?

NEIGHBOR: There is a boy baby in this house, and the Egyptians must be told!

JOCHEBED (*anxiously*): Even if there were, are you so anxious to see another dead Hebrew baby?

NEIGHBOR (*weeping*): They took my child! Why should you have a child if I cannot?

(JOCHEBED *puts a comforting arm around the* NEIGHBOR.)

JOCHEBED: There, there. I understand. Sit here a moment and rest.

NEIGHBOR (*calmer*): Oh, Jochebed, do you truly have a baby boy?

JOCHEBED: Y—yes.

NEIGHBOR: I am sorry. I—I will not tell. It was my grief made me say those wicked things.

JOCHEBED: I know. This is a wicked world.

NEIGHBOR (*earnestly*): How can you hide him? The Egyptians will find out. (*Bitterly*) Better now than later when you grow to love him. It hurts so, then.

JOCHEBED: I know. But Jehovah will help. At least—I cannot give him up now.

NEIGHBOR: May—may I see him?

JOCHEBED: Come.

> (JOCHEBED *takes* NEIGHBOR *off right.* MIRIAM *looks after them. Then she moves the two chairs as if on two sides of a table. Goes stage back and pantomimes meal preparation. While she is busy,* NEIGHBOR *returns.*)

NEIGHBOR: Such a beautiful man-child. I promise not to tell.

> (*She exits left.* MIRIAM *continues with the imaginary meal. Soon,* AMRAM *and* AARON *enter, wearily. Each pulls chair away from the imaginary table and sits, exhausted.*)

MIRIAM: Greetings, Father. Aaron.

AMRAM: A hard day. Tomorrow will be worse. The quota of bricks increases by one hundred.

MIRIAM (*sympathetically*): Oh, Father. Rest now. I will have your dinner soon.

AMRAM: Where is your mother?

MIRIAM: She—she is resting.

AARON (*stands*): The baby? The baby has come?

MIRIAM: Yes.

AMRAM (*hopefully*): A girl?

MIRIAM (*reluctantly*): N–no.

AARON (*angrily*): I *knew* it! A *boy!* You haven't reported it, have you?

(AMRAM *goes off right quickly.*)

MIRIAM: No!

AARON: Are you crazy? You know the law!

MIRIAM (*pleading*): Oh, Aaron, he's so sweet. Such a tiny little thing.

AARON: That tiny little thing is as dangerous as a cobra snake! We must report this at once! (*He starts off left.*)

MIRIAM (*grabs his arm and holds him back*): No, Aaron! No, you can't do it! He's your *brother!*

AARON: He may be my death! Miriam, you know what they do to Hebrews who conceal their boy babies. Do you want to die like that?

MIRIAM: No, but I can't give him up. And Mother *won't!* Oh, Aaron, go look at him.

AARON: No! Better not to see him.

(AMRAM *reenters as* AARON *starts off again.*)

MIRIAM: Aaron, please don't tell!

AMRAM (*sharply*): Aaron! Where are you going?

AARON: To report this boy child to the Egyptians.

AMRAM: No, you will not.

AARON: It is the law!

AMRAM: You will not report this child.

AARON: But the Egyptians—

AMRAM: I am the law here, the head of this house, Aaron!

16

AARON: But, Father—

AMRAM: Don't argue! Your mother wants to try to save him.

AARON: Do you and Mother have the right to risk *our* lives? Miriam's and mine?

MIRIAM: Speak for yourself, Aaron.

AARON (*angrily*): Well, mine, then. Don't I have something to say about that?

AMRAM: No. You are my son. You will *not tell* anyone this new child lives. Do you understand? . . . Aaron, do you understand?

AARON (*sullenly*): Yes!

AMRAM (*gentler*): Don't you want to see your new brother?

AARON: No!

AMRAM: Very well. You needn't look at him. But you cannot give him up to be killed! I, your father, say this.

> (AARON *slumps in a chair. All hold motionless for six seconds. Then* AMRAM *and* AARON *go off left,* MIRIAM *off right. In ten seconds* JOCHEBED *and* MIRIAM *enter right, carrying the basket or box in which they pretend is the baby boy.*)

MIRIAM (*looking in basket*): He looks so sweet.

JOCHEBED: All babies look sweet when they are asleep.

> (AARON *enters left.*)

AARON: What are you doing?

MIRIAM: Trying to save our baby, that's what!

AARON: Just because you haven't been found out for these three months, don't think someone won't tell! The Egyptians will find out!

MIRIAM: Aaron, come look at him.

AARON (*turning away sharply*): No!

JOCHEBED (*gently*): He's your *brother*, Aaron. You never have looked at him.

AARON (*bitterly*): And I never will. Unless it's the day we're found out, and I look in his face and say, "Little brother, I hate you because you kill me!"

JOCHEBED: Aaron!

MIRIAM: Never mind, Mother. Never mind.

JOCHEBED (*after a moment*): All right, Aaron. You needn't look at him. After today, there'll be no chance.

AARON (*turns*): Oh?

MIRIAM: We are taking him away. Mother, is he warm enough?

JOCHEBED: Oh, yes. I'm sure he'll sleep snugly until—Now, you know what to do?

MIRIAM (*almost reciting*): I hide him in the reeds by the pool. The Pharaoh's daughter will come to swim—to swim—

JOCHEBED: As she does every day.

MIRIAM: As she does every day. Then when she sees the baby and wants to keep him—

AARON: What is this silly plot? If you let that baby fall into the hands of Pharaoh's daughter—Mother! Miriam! She'll have him killed!

MIRIAM (*slyly*): I thought you didn't care?

AARON: I *don't*!

JOCHEBED: She won't have him killed. I've heard she is kinder than most Egyptians. She has no husband, no son. He is beautiful. She will keep him. If you'd look at him—

AARON: Take him then! (*He exits left quickly.*)

JOCHEBED: Yes, take him, Miriam. I will pray every minute. Even if we—fail—as Aaron believes—I must know. Come back quickly.

MIRIAM: Yes, Mother.

> (MIRIAM *exits left with the basket and* JOCHEBED *right. After a pause,* AARON *and* AMRAM *enter left.*)

AARON: They're not here! I told you they had this plot.

AMRAM (*calling*): Jochebed! Are you here?

JOCHEBED (*off*): Coming!

> (MIRIAM, *without the basket, enters left as* JOCHEBED *enters right.*)

MIRIAM (*eagerly*): Mother, Mother! It went *well*! Go now. She is expecting you. I ran all the way!

> (JOCHEBED *hurries off left.*)

AMRAM (*calling after her*): Jochebed, come back! Where are you going? Miriam, where is your mother going?

MIRIAM: To Pharaoh's palace, Father.

AMRAM: To Phar—What do you mean?

MIRIAM (*proudly*): Mother is the new nurse to a baby—a baby the princess has adopted. (*happily*) Father—our baby!

AMRAM (*sits down, bewildered*): How did—? Aaron said . . . .

MIRIAM (*contemptuously*): Aaron! You said we couldn't, but we did! I put the basket (*acting out the story*) with the baby in the reeds. Soon the Pharaoh's daughter and her maids came down to swim. Then they woke him up with their chatter. He began to cry. One of the maids found him and took him to the princess! (*to* AARON) I *told* you she'd think he was the prettiest baby she ever saw! "I can't let him die," she said. "I'll keep him!"

AMRAM: She *did*?

MIRIAM: She did! Then I ran out on the path, pretending to chase a butterfly. "Oh, what a nice baby!" I said. I looked in the basket and he—he smiled at me, he did. Then I said, "Are you his mother or his nurse?" One of those maids slapped me, but the princess made her stop. "No, I am not his mother, and I haven't a nurse yet," she said. Then I said, "I bet I could find a nurse among the Hebrew women. But maybe you'd rather have an Egyptian." Then she said, "No, it doesn't matter. If you know someone, send her to me at the palace." So I came for Mother!

AMRAM (*gratefully*): He truly lives, then. Jehovah be praised!

(*They bow their heads in prayer.* JOCHEBED *enters left, smiling.*)

JOCHEBED: Oh, Amram, have you heard?

AMRAM: Miriam was just telling us. Will you be his nurse?

JOCHEBED: Oh, yes! Now he will live and grow up.

AARON: As an Egyptian!

JOCHEBED: As an Egyptian, but alive.

AARON: I'm glad I didn't look at him. When he's grown, he'll be as cruel as any other Egyptian to his own people. Even us.

JOCHEBED: While he is small, I will teach him Jehovah's ways. I will tell him of his heritage.

AARON (*scoffing*): They will take him from a nurse while he is still a little boy. When he is grown, you won't know which Egyptian he is!

JOCHEBED (*with assurance*): Yes, I will. Sometime, somewhere I will hear his name. I will know. Moses. Moses is what she calls him.

AARON: Moses.

MIRIAM: We have a brother named Moses—a prince of Egypt.

20

AARON: I suppose someday you'll say, "Hey, there, Prince Moses, remember me? I'm Miriam, your sister." He will be overjoyed to see his *Hebrew slave sister*!

MIRIAM (*serenely*): Who knows? He just might, at that!

Questions for Talking

1. Was Aaron a coward or was his a sensible fear?

2. Why were the Hebrews slaves? Is there any slavery today?

3. Do you think Aaron really hated Moses? Why?

4. Do boys and girls now sometimes hate their brothers and sisters?

5. Is it possible to hate someone and love him at the same time?

3

The Magician

If you haven't read the Foreword for helpful suggestions, do so now. Playing time is 17 to 21 minutes. Scripture basis is 1 Kings 17. The Bible gives no names for the woman and her son. We chose names. Also, no neighbor is mentioned, but she had some and doubtless they were involved in her story. We imagined one.

The cast may wear biblical dress, ordinary modern clothing, or the modern dress with a biblical headdress. Props needed are: a bowl, wooden spoon, small jug. Place on any available level, as a railing. Also needed, twigs for the "firewood." For staging, place two chairs at left. (Supposedly the bedroom and the widow's home is off left.) Stage right will be where Elijah sits by the brook. The empty center stage is for all other action.

CAST: ELIJAH, *an old prophet of Jehovah;* TIRZAH, *a widow;* MICAH, *her son;* LEAH, *her neighbor;* RACHEL, LEAH's *daughter.*

> (MICAH *slowly enters left. He is weak from hunger. He sinks onto a chair, resting his head on his arms folded on the chair back. After a pause,* TIRZAH, *his mother, enters left. She places a comforting hand on his head.*)

MICAH (*looking up*): I'm sorry, Mother. It is hard to be brave when you are weak and hungry.

TIRZAH (*sadly*): I know, my son, I know. (*She goes center front to look out an imaginary window.*) This barren land. No growing grain. Three years no rain.

MICAH: Jehovah has forgotten us.

TIRZAH (*returning to him*): Micah, Jehovah will provide. Wait and see.

MICAH: You dream, Mother. Three years Jehovah holds back

the rain. Three years because of two enemies: King Ahab and Elijah the prophet.

TIRZAH: King Ahab has done evil in Jehovah's sight. He is being punished.

MICAH: So are we. So are all the people in this land.

TIRZAH: But they say it is Jehovah's will.

MICAH: Why? Why must *we* pay for Ahab's sin?

TIRZAH: Patience, Micah. Somehow Jehovah will provide.

MICAH: When? Will I know what it feels like *not* to be hungry just once before I die?

TIRZAH: Oh, Micah, don't think of food. Put your mind on other things.

MICAH (*stands slowly, clinging to chair for support*): What other things? I am hungry, Mother. Is there nothing to eat, nothing at all?

TIRZAH (*tiredly*): Only a little meal and a small bit of oil. That is all. Enough for two small flat cakes.

MICAH: Then prepare them. Let us eat.

TIRZAH: No. Oh, Micah, I'm saving that until there no longer is hope. Until—the last.

MICAH (*bitterly*): How will you know what is the last? Why do you hope? Do you think the king will send peasants grain?

TIRZAH (*pleading*): Patience a little longer. Jehovah will—

MICAH (*interrupting*): Don't say that again! It is a lie! You delude yourself. Mother, please let us eat what we can.

TIRZAH (*pleading*): Oh, Micah, my son—

MICAH (*going left slowly, giving in*): Never mind. One more bite won't matter—not really—not long. Forget it, Mother. I shall lie down to wait for death. (*He exits left.*)

TIRZAH (*after him*): Micah! Micah! Very well. I'll go fetch wood for a fire. Then I will prepare the last cakes.

> (TIRZAH *goes right, pretends to look for wood, picks up twigs here and there on the floor. She reaches stage right.* ELIJAH *enters, watching her. She continues unaware. Suddenly she sees him and is startled.*)

TIRZAH: Oh!

ELIJAH: Don't be alarmed.

TIRZAH: I didn't hear you. You surprised me, sir.

ELIJAH: Forgive me. I walk quietly, because I must.

TIRZAH (*uneasily*): You—you are in trouble?

ELIJAH (*simply*): My name is Elijah.

TIRZAH (*frightened*): The—the prophet who—who—

ELIJAH: The same.

TIRZAH (*bitterly*): If you are Elijah, do you come to watch us die?

ELIJAH (*sadly*): I want no man's death.

TIRZAH: Then bid the rains come that you stopped. Save the land. If you *are* Elijah!

ELIJAH: I cannot.

TIRZAH: Let the king win!

ELIJAH: I defy him by Jehovah's command.

TIRZAH: You aren't Elijah! You deceive me with false words.

ELIJAH: I am Elijah and I am sent—to you.

TIRZAH (*surprised*): To me?

ELIJAH: I must hide from Ahab's men. I need food. Take me to your home.

TIRZAH (bitterly): Room I have, it's true. Food, no.

ELIJAH: Yet you still live.

TIRZAH: Today, yes. Tomorrow? See these twigs? I gather them to build a fire. Then I will prepare the last bit of our food.

ELIJAH: You have a family?

TIRZAH: One son. I prepare two small cakes of meal. That is all we have. We will eat. Then we will die. Farewell, old man. (*She turns to go.* ELIJAH *stops her.*)

ELIJAH: Wait. Listen to me, daughter. I need a place where the king cannot find me. Hide me in your house. Bake the cakes that I may eat. I faint with hunger.

TIRZAH (*angrily*): Give the last cakes to *you*? Then what of my son?

ELIJAH: In return, I promise your son will eat. You, too, daughter. While I am with you, until the rains come again, the meal will never give out nor the jar of oil run dry.

TIRZAH (*backing away, frightened*): You can—do this? Are you truly Elijah the prophet? Or are you a wizard, a magician?

(LEAH, TIRZAH's *neighbor, enters right, carrying twigs.*)

LEAH: Tirzah! Greetings.

TIRZAH (*relieved*): Leah!

LEAH (*suspiciously*): What is it, Tirzah? Who is this man?

TIRZAH (*nervously*): He—he says he is—the prophet, Elijah.

LEAH (*afraid*): Elijah? Truly?

TIRZAH: I—am not sure. He talks likes a magician or wizard.

LEAH (*braver*): Well, if he is Elijah, he's the cause of all our trouble.

ELIJAH: No, daughter.

LEAH: If you are Elijah, then you hold back the rain and bring drought to the land.

ELIJAH: Only because of the wickedness of King Ahab. By the word of Jehovah.

TIRZAH: Will nothing please Jehovah except the death of my only son?

ELIJAH: You heard what I said before. Take me home with you.

LEAH (*surprised*): He wants to go to your house?

TIRZAH: Yes.

LEAH: No, Tirzah! What if he *is* a magician? Or, even if he is Elijah—the king seeks him to kill him! You will die, too, for sheltering the king's enemy!

TIRZAH: At least the sword is swifter than starvation.

ELIJAH: My daughter, I promise you will not starve.

LEAH (*jeering*): Are you reading signs in the sky? Tirzah, don't be gullible. He *must* be a magician. Have nothing to do with him. Bid him go!

TIRZAH: He—he says, as long as he is in our house, the oil will not cease nor the meal give out!

LEAH (*impressed*): He said that? (*She looks him over carefully.*) Tirzah, do you believe him?

TIRZAH: I don't know.

LEAH (*she looks at him again, then makes a complete about-face in attitude*): Do as he asks, Tirzah! Take him home with you!

TIRZAH: Leah!

LEAH: Feed him! Surely so great a prophet speaks the truth. Do it, Tirzah!

TIRZAH (*bewildered*): But—but, Leah just now you said he might be a magician.

LEAH (*lightly*): Magician or prophet, who cares? Take him, Tirzah!

TIRZAH: But, Leah—

LEAH: Don't forget, in days to come when you are—*prosperous*—don't forget your friends! Remember who they are!

> (LEAH *exits right.* TIRZAH *looks at* ELIJAH *a moment, then speaks doubtfully.*)

TIRZAH: I suppose, if you are deceiving me, the bit of food will not prevent our starving. But if you truly are the prophet, who knows? Come!

> (TIRZAH *and* ELIJAH *go slowly left to her "house."*)

TIRZAH (*calling*): Micah! Micah!

MICAH (*weakly, off*): Yes, Mother.

TIRZAH: Micah, come here. (*To* ELIJAH) Sit down. (*He does and seems to be praying.* MICAH *enters, leans weakly on the other chair.*) Micah, this man says he is the prophet Elijah.

MICAH: Elijah? Here? Is it true?

TIRZAH: I don't know.

MICAH: If he is Elijah, why does he come here?

TIRZAH: He says—to hide from King Ahab in our house. He wants us to—feed him, too.

MICAH (*bitterly*): *Feed* him? If he is Elijah, then it is his fault we have nothing left. He asks for the last of—nothing.

TIRZAH: He—he says if we give him our food, he will not let the meal or the oil run out!

MICAH: It may be a trick.

TIRZAH: I know. Oh, Micah, my son! (*She begins weeping into her hands.*) What shall I do? If I take the last of the meal and give to a stranger—oh, my son, what am I doing to you?

MICAH (*comes, puts his hand on her shoulder*): Don't cry, Mother. He is an old man. Make him the cakes.

TIRZAH: Whether he is Elijah or not?

MICAH: Whether he is Elijah or not. Don't cry anymore, Mother.

(*She dries her eyes. He sits in the other chair, leaning back weakly.* ELIJAH *continues his silent praying.* TIRZAH *busies herself, going through the motions of making an imaginary fire, mixing imaginary ingredients. She cooks as if making pancakes. The audience watches the pantomime. When they are ready, she brings the imaginary cakes to* ELIJAH. *Then she turns and gives one to* MICAH.)

TIRZAH (*shaking his shoulder, waking him*): Micah! Micah!

MICAH (*rousing, weakly*): Yes, Mother?

TIRZAH: Here, my son, eat! (*He slowly eats the imaginary cake in two bites and then drops off to sleep again. Meanwhile,* TIRZAH *does go to* ELIJAH.) Here is a cake, sir. Whether or not you are Elijah—here is the last cake.

(ELIJAH *takes it, looks at it a moment.*)

ELIJAH: Why do you not prepare one for yourself?

TIRZAH: With air? The meal and the oil are gone.

ELIJAH: Are you sure?

TIRZAH: I emptied the vessels myself!

ELIJAH (*gently*): Look again, daughter. Go! . . . Go!

(*Reluctantly,* TIRZAH *returns to the bowl and jug as if humoring an old man. She looks into the bowl, looks away, then quickly looks back. Then she quickly looks into the jug. Agitated, she turns to* ELIJAH.)

TIRZAH (*frightened*): There's *meal!* There's *oil!*

ELIJAH: I told you.

TIRZAH: But I used it all! What magic is this?

ELIJAH: Prepare a cake for yourself.

TIRZAH: No, no! I will prepare another for Micah. You see how weak he is!

ELIJAH: Prepare one for Micah and for yourself. And for me. The meal and oil will not give out. I promise. Now I will rest. (*He seems to sleep in the chair.*)

>(TIRZAH *begins mixing, excitedly. She is interrupted by the entrance from the right of* LEAH *and her daughter,* RACHEL.)

LEAH (*keeping her voice down*): I see you brought him home, Tirzah. Rachel, speak to Tirzah.

RACHEL (*loudly*): Greetings, Tirzah!

LEAH: Sh–h–h! Not so loud!

TIRZAH: You won't believe it! Look, Leah! (*She shows the bowl and jug to them.*)

LEAH: Only that much left? Well, it will make two small cakes.

TIRZAH (*excitedly*): It already has made two small cakes!

LEAH: Then you had more oil and meal than you knew.

TIRZAH: No! I used it *all*. But here it is again! Look—I will bake the cakes. (*She seems to cook as on a griddle, while the guests watch, with side glances at the sleeping* ELIJAH. TIRZAH *gives an imaginary cake to each of the guests.*)

RACHEL (*tasting*): It's good.

LEAH (*tasting*): It's real!

TIRZAH (*happily*): Yes! Now look here. (*She shows vessels to* LEAH.) I used it all. But here it is *again*.

LEAH (*awed, looking over at* ELIJAH): He does work magic! It is witchcraft.

TIRZAH (*troubled*): No, Leah, not—witchcraft.

LEAH: Who cares, as long as it's food.

>(ELIJAH *rouses and watches them.*)

TIRZAH (*troubled*): But I cannot—yet he must be a magician. Look at the meal.

LEAH: Tirzah, give me meal and oil. My family needs food, too. I'm your friend. The least you can do is share. If you do, I won't tell. But if you don't—

ELIJAH (*rising, speaks loudly*): Woman! Do you threaten?

LEAH (*backing off, frightened*): Oh, no, Sir Magician!

ELIJAH (*to Tirzah*): Give her enough for today. Now, listen to me, woman. If you tell where you got the meal, or reveal that I am here, crows will pick out your eyes! Do you hear?

RACHEL (*clinging to* LEAH): Mother—r—r—r!

ELIJAH: Do you hear, woman?

LEAH (*frightened*): I hear!

ELIJAH: What of this girl?

LEAH: She will say nothing! (*Shakes Rachel.*) Speak up, girl!

RACHEL (*tearfully*): I won't talk!

ELIJAH: Go, then. At mealtimes, come for your share. Otherwise, stay out!

LEAH: Yes! Come, Rachel! (*They leave quickly.* TIRZAH *has been a frightened observer.*)

ELIJAH: Good riddance. Why do you stand there? Are you afraid?

TIRZAH: Y—yes.

ELIJAH (*gently*): I will not hurt your neighbor. But she doesn't know that. Threats will keep her silent. Ahab must not know that I am here. It is the Lord's will.

TIRZAH: Y—yes.

ELIJAH (*impatiently*): Woman, I *am* Elijah! Do you still doubt?

TIRZAH (*tearfully*): I, I don't know, sir.

(Micah *stirs in the chair.*)

Micah (*weakly*): Mother . . . Mother . . . I hurt. (Tirzah *runs to him, feels his forehead.*)

Tirzah (*alarmed*): Micah, you are so hot. Come, my son, let me help you to your bed.

> (*She ad-libs as she helps him up and partially lifts him off left.* Elijah *watches them go. He sits in the chair and is brought to his feet by a loud scream, off, from* Tirzah.)

Elijah (*calls*): What is the matter, woman?

Tirzah (*off, frantically*): He isn't breathing! Micah isn't breathing! (Elijah *goes off left as she continues*) Oh, Micah, my son, my son! Don't die! Don't die!

Elijah (*off*): Go! Leave me with him.

Tirzah (*off*): He's dead! Micah is dead!

Elijah (*off*): Go, woman! Wait. And pray.

> (Tirzah *reenters, pacing frantically.*)

Tirzah: Oh, what can I do? What can I do? Jehovah, spare my son! He is so young. Life is so hard. Spare my son! Oh, Micah, Micah! First your sister, then your father. Now you. Why not me, O Jehovah? Why not *me*? I cannot bear it! Oh, oh, oh—(*She sinks to floor by a chair, cradling her head on her arms, weeping. After a pause,* Elijah *reenters, assisting* Micah, *who is still weak but obviously stronger.*)

Micah: Mother.

> (Tirzah *looks up amazed. Slowly she rises, touches* Micah, *then folds him in her arms.*)

Tirzah: Micah! . . . Thank you, Lord! (*In a moment she helps him sit down.* Elijah *has watched.*)

Tirzah (*to* Elijah, *awestruck*): I don't understand. I have seen death many times. Micah was *dead*. I *know* he was dead!

31

ELIJAH: Yes.

TIRZAH (*seeing the truth*): You are no magician. You truly are the man of God—Elijah.

ELIJAH: I told you.

TIRZAH (*humbly*): I did not believe. Not really. Forgive me. (*She kneels.*)

ELIJAH (*assisting her to stand*): Stand, my daughter. Kneel only to Jehovah. He it is who restored your son. I am only his servant.

TIRZAH: (*bowing*): You honor us.

ELIJAH (*lightly*): Well, now that we understand each other, I find I need something.

TIRZAH: Anything.

ELIJAH: Then why don't you prepare some of those good cakes for Micah and me? We both are hungry.

Questions for Talking

1. Do droughts still bring famine in the world?

2. What are other reasons for hunger in the world?

3. Is there a connection between hunger today and the reason for hunger in the play?

4. What do you think of these characters? Do you like Leah? Was she a good friend to Tirzah? Why?

5. Why was Tirzah so hard to convince that Elijah was Elijah?

6. Do people blame God for their troubles? Have you heard them?

4

Winners Can Be Losers

If you haven't read the Foreword for helpful suggestions, do so now. Playing time is 20 to 23 minutes. Scripture basis is 2 Kings 5:1–19. Imaginary characters are added where such seemed logical. Names not given in the Bible have been added, also. Our play ends before Gehazi's fate was told, simply because that is another story.

Biblical costumes may be worn or modern clothing with biblical headdresses. For staging, one chair is needed, with the adding of a throw covering when it is a throne in "Israel." A tall staff for the CHAMBERLAIN *and a scroll for the* KING OF ISRAEL *are props needed. The one chair is at left when the play begins.*

The play is in three segments. At the times of the changes, rehearse the movements in darkness so the lights are off only a couple of seconds. You lose an audience rapidly in darkness.

CAST: NAAMAN, *commander of the armies of Syria;* NAARAH, *his wife;* TAL, *Naaman's steward;* MERAB, *a Hebrew slave girl;* KING OF SYRIA; CHAMBERLAIN *to the king of Syria;* KING OF ISRAEL; *girl* SERVANT *to king of Israel;* GEHAZI, *servant to Elisha;* ELISHA, *the prophet. If you have extra boys and girls who want to act with no lines to speak, add servants for the kings and soldiers for the kings and Naaman.*

> (*As the play opens,* TAL, *the chief steward and servant to* NAAMAN, *enters right, calling.*)

TAL: Merab! . . . Merab, where are you? (*muttering*) Never can find that girl when I want her. Merab!

> (MERAB *runs in breathlessly from left.*)

MERAB: Here I am, Tal!

> (TAL *shakes her.*)

33

TAL: Merab, where have you been?

MERAB: I—I was playing with the new kittens. Please, Tal, may I have one for my own? Please?

TAL: (*sharply*): You may not. Remember you are a slave, and a slave has nothing of her own.

MERAB (*sadly*): I forgot.

TAL (*scolding*): You also forgot to clean and burnish your mistress' sandals. If those kittens make you neglect your duties—well, I may have to dispose of them all.

MERAB (*clutching his hand*): You wouldn't. Oh, Tal, please. I will be good. Please, Tal, don't kill the little kittens. They are so soft and sweet. Please, Tal!

TAL: Oh, all right. But, next time—

MERAB: I'll be good. You'll see. Not the kittens.

TAL (*sits in chair*): Merab, come here. (*She stands beside him.*) This is a troubled house. You don't help us by disobeying.

MERAB: I'm sorry.

TAL: You must learn to behave like a proper slave.

MERAB: It's so hard to remember I'm a slave. I keep thinking of when I was home in Israel . . .

TAL (*interrupting*): You aren't in Israel. You never will be in Israel again. You are in Syria, a slave in the house of Naaman, commander of the king's armies. Keep thinking that.

MERAB (*bitterly*): Naaman killed my father and mother!

TAL (*shakes her*): No such thing! That was *war*. They were *victims*. Don't say that again.

MERAB (*with spirit*): Well, somebody killed them—from Naaman's army. Now, Jehovah punishes him, and I'm *glad!* I'm glad!

TAL (*jumping up*): You are a wicked girl! A good beating will teach you to curb your tongue. Come with me. (*He begins dragging her right.*)

MERAB (*resisting, crying*): No! No, Tal, no! Not again.

> (NAARAH, *wife of* NAAMAN, *enters right.*)

NAARAH (*wearily*): Tal, Merab! What is the matter?

> (TAL *releases* MERAB, *who runs and falls down at her mistress' feet.*)

MERAB: Don't let him beat me again. Please, mistress, I'll be good!

NAARAH: Hush, Merab. Tal, what is it?

TAL: This Hebrew slave is impudent, disobedient, and calls down evil upon my master.

NAARAH (*sadly*): I doubt if more evil could be called down. Let her go this time, Tal. She is a child. I will talk to her.

TAL: If you say so, mistress. May I be excused?

NAARAH: Yes, Tal. (*He exits right.*) Merab, why do you cross Tal? He is a good man.

MERAB (*rising, wiping tears away*): I—I don't know.

NAARAH: When you obey, does he ever mistreat you?

MERAB: No, mistress.

NAARAH: Then why do you disobey? You are treated better here in this house than slaves are in other houses.

MERAB (*desperately*): But, mistress, I'm still a slave. I don't want to be a slave!

NAARAH: Nonsense. I'll hear no more. Go do what Tal bids.

MERAB (*sadly*): Yes, mistress. (*She leaves right, looking back once at her mistress.*)

(NAARAH *walks downstage, looks out imaginary window. In a moment,* NAAMAN *enters left, slowly. His face is pale and sad. His hands are swathed in bandages. He stops when he notices* NAARAH.)

NAAMAN: Naarah.

NAARAH (*turning to him*): Naaman!

NAAMAN (*warning her off*): Don't come near me.

NAARAH: I am not afraid.

NAAMAN (*bitterly*): Do you think I want to give my death to you?

NAARAH (*touching his bandaged hands*): My husband, I will share your burden if the gods will it.

NAAMAN (*moving away*): No, Naarah. Oh, that I had the courage to take my life before I become—loathsome.

NAARAH: Don't say that, Naaman. Don't think it. Surely somewhere there is a cure. The gods—

NAAMAN (*interrupting*): The gods! Don't you know I am dying? The gods can't stop this slow death.

NAARAH: Come, Naaman. Let me take you to your room. I will rub your forehead, and you shall rest. The king comes today. He must not see you in such despair.

NAAMAN: Why does he come? He can do nothing.

NAARAH (*leading him off right*): Lean on me. I will help you. Do not fear to touch me. I am not afraid.

(*They leave. Immediately* MERAB *enters right, looking behind her. She tiptoes left. Just as she reaches the exit,* TAL *enters right.*)

TAL: Merab!

MERAB (*stopping guiltily*): Oh!

TAL: The kittens again?

MERAB: I cleaned the sandals! I put everything away. Nothing is left undone.

TAL: The kittens must wait. Your mistress will be needing you. She must dress to welcome the king.

MERAB: Why is the king coming here?

TAL: To persuade Naaman to go to Egypt.

MERAB: Egypt?

TAL: A great seer lives in Egypt. He may be able to cure our master of his leprosy.

MERAB: There is a great seer in Samaria. Elisha. *He* can cure Naaman.

TAL (*unbelieving*): Oh?

MERAB: It's *so!* The mantle of the great Elijah fell on his shoulders!

TAL: I've heard of the great Elijah.

MERAB: Elisha works miracles, too.

TAL: Such as?

MERAB: 'Tis said the waters of the Jordan parted for him. Once he made a pot of oil to fill again and again. He even made the dead live again. Other miracles, too.

TAL: You think he might be able to make our master well?

MERAB: If Elisha wishes.

TAL: Merab, go tell Naaman.

MERAB (*frightened*): No! I'm afraid of him. (*Begins weeping in her hands.*) Please don't make me go! Not Naaman.

TAL (*gently*): Never mind. Go see if your mistress needs help.

(*She runs off right. In a moment* NAARAH *enters right.*)

NAARAH: Tal, is all ready for the king?

TAL: Yes, mistress. Mistress, did you see Merab?

NAARAH: She passed me in the hall, crying. What is it, Tal?

TAL: She told me a strange tale about a Hebrew holy man. He works miracles.

NAARAH: You think—?

TAL: Mistress, let me call the child. She will tell you herself.

> (*She nods. He runs off and returns pulling the unwilling* MERAB.)

TAL: Now, Merab, tell our mistress what you told me. Don't be frightened. No one will eat you!

MERAB: I just said Elisha could cure anybody! He even raised one from the dead.

NAARAH (*urgently*): How, girl? Does he cast spells? Is he a physician?

MERAB (*frightened*): I don't know, mistress. He—he's something special with—with Jehovah God!

TAL: Jehovah is the Hebrew God. He is invisible.

NAARAH: I know.

> (*They are interrupted. The* CHAMBERLAIN *of the* KING OF SYRIA *enters left. He stops. With a tall staff he knocks three times on the floor.*)

CHAMBERLAIN: The king of Syria!

> (*The* KING *enters left and comes center.* TAL *kneels at the same time pulling down* MERAB *until she is prostrate.* NAARAH *curtsies deeply. The* KING *takes* NAARAH'S *hand and assists her to rise.* TAL *and* MERAB *rise also.* MERAB *hides behind* TAL.)

SYRIA: Lady Naarah.

NAARAH: My lord.

SYRIA: Where is my commander? How is he today?

NAARAH: In poor spirits, my lord. He despairs of life and longs for death.

SYRIA: We shall send him to Egypt at once.

NAARAH: My lord, we have been listening to this child. Come, Merab! The king will not hurt you. (*A frightened* MERAB *steps from behind* TAL.) There is a holy man nearer than Egypt.

SYRIA: Oh? Where?

NAARAH: Speak up, Merab.

MERAB (*nervously*): In—in Samaria. (*She hides behind* TAL.)

TAL (*bowing low*): May I speak, my lord?

SYRIA: Indeed. Someone needs to.

TAL: The child is frightened, my lord. She is a slave from Israel. She tells of the miracles done by one Elisha. He is a prophet, successor to the great Elijah.

SYRIA: I have heard tales of Elijah, the prophet.

TAL: This Elisha's miracles are such—well, my mistress believes he might cure the commander.

SYRIA (*walking around to* MERAB): What do you think, young slave? Speak up. What do you think?

MERAB (*sulkily*): It isn't a slave's place to think!

NAARAH: Merab! Tal, take her out and whip her!

TAL: Pardon, my lady. She meant the king no offense. It is simply—she blames the commander for the death of her parents.

MERAB (*with spirit*): He did! He killed them!

SYRIA: That is war, child. You are too young to understand.

MERAB: But not too young to be an orphan. And a slave.

TAL: *That will do!* Excuse me, Mistress, my lord! (*He pulls* MERAB *off left.*)

NAARAH: I ask pardon, my lord. She has yet to learn how to be a slave.

SYRIA: It is nothing. Now, about the holy man—

(NAAMAN *enters right. He bows low before the* KING.)

SYRIA: Greetings, my friend. We are discussing your fate.

NAAMAN: My fate is sealed.

SYRIA: Perhaps. Perhaps not. At least it is worth a chance. Naaman, prepare for a journey.

NAAMAN: My lord, a trip to Egypt is useless.

SYRIA: Not Egypt. To Israel. I'll put the whole thing on the King of Israel. (*Beckons to waiting* CHAMBERLAIN.) Let us go and prepare a letter. Then you will send it ahead. (CHAMBERLAIN *bows and steps aside as the* KING *starts off left*). Be ready to leave in the morning. Oh, and take that little Hebrew spitfire along. A dose of seeing her conquered country may be good for her.

(*He exits left, followed by* CHAMBERLAIN.) NAARAH *helps* NAAMAN *off right, followed by* TAL. *Lights off. In the darkness, move the chair to center back and cover.* KING OF ISRAEL *sits. Lights on again. The king's* SERVANT *is entering left, a scroll in her hand. She kneels before him. He takes it. She stands aside, waiting. He reads a bit, then jumps up, agitated. He is a comic character and overacts all through.*)

ISRAEL: What! Naaman coming here again? (*Rushes about erratically.*) Oh, dear! Oh, dear! What shall I do? (*To* SERVANT) Who brought this letter?

SERVANT: A messenger. Just now, my lord.

ISRAEL (*groaning*): When will the scourge of Israel arrive? When? When? When?

SERVANT: Perhaps the letter says.

ISRAEL: Oh? Oh, yes. (*Reads*) Immediately! He is here! What does he want now? *All* of Israel? Oh, dear! Oh, dear!

SERVANT: The letter.

ISRAEL: Yes, yes. (*Reads*) Leprosy! I can't cure leprosy! (*Thrusts scroll at* SERVANT, *paces, wringing hands.*) Does he think I am God? When he finds I can do nothing, is this war again? Oh, woe is me! Woe is me! Would that Jehovah let this leprosy kill him before he sets foot in the palace! What shall I do? Oh, what shall I do?

> (*During the above, the* SERVANT *has seen* GEHAZI, *the servant of Elisha, enter left. He whispers to* GEHAZI, *then returns and kneels before the* KING.)

ISRAEL (*noticing him*): What is it? What is it now?

SERVANT: Gehazi, my lord. The servant of the prophet Elisha.

ISRAEL: Oh, no! Not now—not now. I have enough trouble with that prophet when I don't have other trouble, but when I have trouble from Syria and trouble from Elisha, I have *trouble*! Woe is me!

SERVANT: It is about Naaman, my lord.

ISRAEL: Why didn't you say so? (*To* GEHAZI) Come here. Speak up.

GEHAZI (*bowing*): O King, my master, Elisha, bids me say to you: "Do not despair. Send Naaman to me. There is a prophet in Israel."

> (*At this moment, the king's* SERVANT *runs left and then onstage again, bowing and ushering in* NAAMAN, NAA-RAH, TAL, MERAB, *and any other walk-on soldiers or servants. It is an orderly entrance.*)

SERVANT: The Lord Naaman, my lord!

ISRAEL (*running to meet him, pretending excessive joy, over-acting*): Welcome! Welcome! Thrice welcome, great Naaman!

NAAMAN: Don't come too near. I am unclean. I have leprosy.

ISRAEL (*backing off nervously*): N–no. I mean, y–yes. I mean I know. I mean the King of Syria sent word.

NAAMAN: Well?

ISRAEL (*nervously*): Yes, thank you. I am quite well.

NAAMAN (*impatiently*): Not you! What can you do for me?

ISRAEL: N–nothing. I can do nothing.

NAAMAN (*losing temper*): Nothing? (*To his people*) You see? I told you this was a foolish trip. Let us return to Damascus at once!

GEHAZI (*interrupting, bowing low*): My lord, wait! I come to greet you from the prophet Elisha.

TAL (*to* NAAMAN): Elisha is the one the maid spoke of! Merab, come, come. (*She comes reluctantly.*) Tell our master.

NAAMAN: Speak up, girl. This is the same one?

MERAB: Y–yes.

NAAMAN (*to* GEHAZI): What of Elisha then?

GEHAZI: My master bids you come to him in Samaria.

NAAMAN: Samaria? (*He turns away, discouraged. He is disappointed. All watch him. In a moment he turns to his people.*) I did not know till now. I–hoped. No, I will not go. Why should there be more–hope–in Israel or Samaria, than in Syria? Let us return home.

NAARAH: Please, Naaman! You have come this far. Merab, tell him again about the miracles. Tell him!

MERAB (*grudgingly*): There–there were miracles. (*She stops.*)

NAARAH: Oh, that girl! Naaman, please. For me? Please?

NAAMAN (*after a moment, sighing*): All right. To please you. Even though it is useless.

(*Lights off. Remove the chair in darkness.* KING OF
ISRAEL, SERVANT *and any other of his group leave. Those
remaining regroup for a new look. Lights on.*)

GEHAZI (*going off right*): Wait. I will tell my master you are
here. (*Off right.*)

NAAMAN (*gloomily*): I wish I had not come. All is useless.

NAARAH: Don't lose hope, my husband.

TAL: This is a great and holy man.

GEHAZI (*returning*): My master, Elisha, says—

NAAMAN (*sharply*): Where is your master?

GEHAZI: He—he sent *me* out to say his words.

NAAMAN (*enraged*): What! I come all this way. I, commander of
all the armies of Syria—and this—this *prophet* cannot even
come out to me?

NAARAH: Naaman!

NAAMAN: Come! We will return to Syria.

NAARAH (*holding him back*): No! Don't go. Listen to the
prophet's words. For *me*, Naaman! (NAAMAN *stops.*)

GEHAZI: My master says, "Bid Naaman go dip seven times in
Jordan, and he will be clean."

NAAMAN (*he stares at the servant then is angry, pacing back and
forth*): For this I come to a—a *desert*! To hear the words
of a backwoods prophet. Not in person! Through a servant.
"Dip in Jordan." That muddy stream? We have better rivers
in Damascus. Let us go.

TAL: Master, listen. It is so easy a thing to do.

MERAB (*grudgingly*): Jordan isn't far. Over there (*pointing left*).

TAL: If the prophet had told you to do something hard, would
you not have *tried*? This is so easy.

NAARAH: Please do as he says, Naaman.

TAL: Master, you cannot be made worse by this Jordan. Merab, tell him about Jordan.

MERAB (*unwillingly*): 'Tis said once Elijah divided the waters of Jordan.

NAARAH: Listen, Naaman. Listen.

TAL: Surely, after coming so far, you will not be stopped because the final act is so simple? (TAL *and* NAARAH *watch him pleadingly. He thinks.*)

NAAMAN: Very well. I will go. Gehazi will show the way. Tal, come with me. Naarah, remain here.

NAARAH: Yes, Naaman.

> (*Only the three leave left. All others who may be in the Syrian party remain. They watch after the departing three. Then the servants rest. Ad-lib conversation creatively. The tempo is slow, waiting.*)

NAARAH (*after a wait*): I was so afraid he'd say no.

MERAB (*not really caring*): He nearly did.

NAARAH (*after thought*): The prophet's not appearing—that was a blow to Naaman's pride. I wonder why the holy man only sent out word?

MERAB: Perhaps to teach the commander a lesson.

NAARAH: What lesson?

MERAB: That a victor does not always win. That Jehovah is no respecter of persons. That he is the Most High God.

> (*They wait silently. Then* GEHAZI *runs in from the left.*)

GEHAZI: He comes! (*He runs on to right to* ELISHA. *All on stage surge left eagerly. In a moment* TAL *enters.*)

TAL: Mistress! Look! (NAAMAN *enters, the bandages gone, his hands out before him. He goes to* NAARAH.)

NAAMAN: Look! All the spots are gone. I can touch you again. (*To all*) I am clean once more. Where is the prophet? He must come see!

(ELISHA, *followed by* GEHAZI, *enters right.*)

ELISHA: I am here.

NAAMAN (*kneeling before him*): O prophet, how can I thank you for the great gift I have received?

ELISHA: It was not I, but Jehovah. And your own obedience and faith.

NAAMAN (*rising*): I know now, there is no God on earth but the God of Israel. I must pay in some way. Ask of me any treasure!

ELISHA: I want nothing.

NAAMAN: Grant me a boon, then. Let me take back with me earth from near Jordan. Upon it, I will kneel and offer sacrifice to the God of Israel.

ELISHA: Take it and go in peace.

(ELISHA *raises his hand in blessing. Then he and* GEHAZI *leave right.*)

NAAMAN: If only there were something I could do. I feel within me the need to do something.

TAL: Master, the child, Merab. Perhaps you will free her? She may have people in Israel.

NAARAH: After all, she is the one who told us of the prophet.

NAAMAN: Merab, come here. (*She stands before him.*) Child, I can never repay my debt to you. Do you want to stay here?

MERAB (*sadly*): I have no people left, so where would I go? It is better to remain a slave in Syria than to die in Israel.

NAAMAN (*putting his hand on her shoulder*): Then you shall return with us. But not as a slave. From this moment you are no longer slave or servant, but a daughter. As a token, what gift shall I give you? Anything! Name it.

MERAB (*timidly*): May I have—have a—a *kitten*?

> (*All laugh in joy.* NAAMAN, *arm across* MERAB's *shoulder, leads them off left.*)

NAAMAN: You may have all the kittens! I foresee cats all over the place. Let's all go home!

Questions for Talking

1. What do you think of these characters? Talk about each one.

2. Is there leprosy now? Is it curable?

3. Did Naaman kill Merab's parents?

4. Was Merab treated well? If the answer is yes, why was she unhappy? Was this foolish?

5. What does the word "freedom" mean to you?

6. Do you think Naaman would have accepted the prophet's command if his task had been more difficult?

7. Is it hard to accept favors without returning them?

8. What is gratitude?

5

The Man Who Said No to God

If you haven't read the Foreword for helpful suggestions, do so now. Playing time 20 to 23 minutes. Scripture basis: the book of Jonah. Note that the Mediterranean was known as the Great Sea, and Tarshish was on the eastern coast of Iberia, present-day Spain. In a Bible encyclopedia look up "casting lots." The Bible gives no name for the captain. We chose ABDEEL.

No special costumes are needed. A cap for the captain and a crown for the king will be enough. However, if the cast wishes to create costumes, let them.

To stage the play place risers, or chairs, or stools, or even a ladder at stage right. This will be where the STORYTELLERS *assemble casually. The remainder of the playing area is bare.*

What about some sound effects for the storm? For the thunder a piece of sheet tin shaken is perfect. For the wind sound, use a tape recorder and experiment. Hold the microphone close to the mouth and breathe in while shaping and reshaping the lips (something like a backward whistle). By varying the volume of the tape you get a good wind sound. For the lightning, flicker the room lights or spotlights, if you use them.

Events on the ship and in the streets of Nineveh are imaginary but quite probable.

PRONUNCIATION GUIDE: *Chemosh, god of Moab =* kē-mōsh′; *Molech, god of the Ammonites =* mō′-lĕk; *Dagon, god of Philistia =* dā′-gŏn; *Osiris, god in Egypt =* ō-sī′-ris; *Isis, goddess of Egypt =* ī′sis.

CAST: JONAH *and eight* STORYTELLERS. STORYTELLERS *1,2,5,6 are girls and 3,4,7,8 are boys. The device used in which several people speak as one is called by such names as choral speaking, verse choir, or concert speech. To be effective, it must be as expressive and sparkling as if only one person, an expressive person, was saying it. The director will find places for the* STORY-

TELLERS *to use movement and gestures, sometimes even all together.*

> (STORYTELLERS *enter right, take casual positions on their levels. They speak together.*)

STORYTELLERS: We're here to tell you a story.

No. 1 (*to others, objecting*): Not just a *story*. It could happen. It did.

No. 2: She's right.

No. 1: Even if it does sound strange.

STORYTELLERS: We all will tell the story. So just call us the Storytellers.

No. 2: That makes sense! What else?

No. 3 (*stepping out*): Except when we become *actors*. (*Strutting proudly*) Once I play the captain of a ship. A *very* fine fellow I am! (*returns to place*)

STORYTELLERS (*mockingly*): Ha!

No. 4: *I'll* be the king of Assyria and wear a crown!

No. 5 (*quickly*): I'll be a citizen in Nineveh, that wicked city.

No. 6: Me, too.

No. 7: In the first part, I am a sailor. Later I'll be a citizen in Nineveh, that wicked city.

No. 8: So will I.

STORYTELLERS: So we are both Storytellers and actors. You, the audience, are in it, too.

No. 6: Your imaginations will supply the ship, the city street, the palace—all the scenery and props we need.

No. 7 (*gleefully waving hand*): Except the gourd vine!

No. 8 (*also waving*): And the cutworm!

Nos. 7 & 8: We play the gourd vine and the cutworm—with the help of your imaginations.

STORYTELLERS: So let's get on with our story of "The Man Who Said No to God."

No. 1 (*to others*): He shouldn't have done it!

No. 2 (*to No. 1*): Then there wouldn't be a story.

No. 1 (*shrugs*): Okay, then.

STORYTELLERS: A long time ago, seven or eight hundred years before Christ, there lived a man named Jonah.

No. 2 (*to audience*): There he is now.

(JONAH *enters left and stands center, closed.*)

STORYTELLERS: Jonah was a prophet. His father was a prophet before him. They lived in a small village near Bethlehem.

No. 3: Called Gath-hepher.

No. 4: Who cares?

No. 3: I do because I can *say* it. Gath-hepher. Gath-hepher.

No. 4: Marvelous! But wait. Before we go too far, should we say something about Nineveh?

STORYTELLERS: There was a city in our story, the heart of the problem: Nineveh, the capital of Assyria. Nineveh, nearly six hundred miles from Gath-hepher.

No. 4: Across dangerous country—

No. 5: Inhabited by warlike people.

No. 7 (*thoughtfully*): Now Nineveh was a wicked city.

No. 8: Very, very wicked.

STORYTELLERS: The word of the Lord came to Jonah, son of Amittai: (*calling out*) Jo-o–onah! . . . Jonah!

(JONAH *turns slowly, falls to his knees. After a pause,* STORYTELLERS *continue.*)

Arise, Jonah. There is work to do.

JONAH (*rises, looks up*): Yes, Lord?

STORYTELLERS: Go to Nineveh in Assyria—

JONAH (*shocked*): Nineveh? That wicked city?

STORYTELLERS (*sternly*): Go to Nineveh! Proclaim in the streets: "Thus says Jehovah God: 'I have seen your wickedness. I, God of gods, proclaim your destruction for your wickedness.'" Go, Jonah.

> (*When the voices cease,* JONAH *stands still a moment. Then he looks around carefully.*)

JONAH: Lord? . . . Lord? . . . (*relieved*) He's gone! (*thinking*) To Nineveh? . . . I am afraid. . . . If I go, those wicked Assyrians—those wicked, bloodthirsty people—they will kill me! . . . Our God means nothing to them! . . . They won't listen to his prophet. They will kill his prophet! . . . I can see my head now on the walls of Nineveh! *I can't!* . . . I will run away!

> (JONAH *runs off left.*)

STORYTELLERS: So Jonah, the Lord's prophet, said no to God. He went first to Joppa, a port on the Great Sea.

(No. 3 *puts on his captain's cap, goes center. Nos. 4,7,8 become "sailors." The girls, Nos. 1,2,5,6 remain in place.*)

No. 3: Look lively, men! Secure that line, sailor. (No. 7 *plays out a length of imaginary rope and pretends to recoil it again.*)
Hoist the jib! We'll catch the tide. (No. 8 *seems to be hauling up a small sail.* JONAH *runs in.*)

JONAH (*panicky*): Where is the captain of this vessel?

No. 3: I am Captain Abdeel of the good ship *West Wind.*

JONAH: Where bound, captain?

No. 3: To Tarshish. As far as man may go across the Great Sea—to the land of the Iberians.

JONAH: Will you take a passenger?

No. 3: For money, yes.

JONAH (*handing him imaginary money*): Is this enough? (*The captain looks but doesn't answer.* JONAH *holds out more.*)

No. 3 (*taking imaginary money*): That will do. (*Curious*) No one goes to Tarshish. Why do you?

JONAH: That's my business! . . . I'm tired. . . . Where may I rest?

No. 3: (*shrugs*): Below. There are bunks. Help yourself.

>(JONAH *goes upstage left, sits on floor, leans against wall and "sleeps."*)

No. 3: All hands, lively! Up anchor. Loose the lines! Lift the mainsail. Man the sweeps!

>(*The "sailors" carry out orders. Then they all freeze. No. 6 comes front center.*)

No. 6: The ship was well out to sea. No clouds in the sky. No change in the wind. Then, suddenly, out of nowhere, a strange, violent storm. (*She returns to her place.*)

>(*Sound effects of storm begin: wind, thunder. Lights flicker. Make the storm so noisy the players have to shout to be heard over the noise. Let it continue throughout the following. The sailors cry out over the increasing noise.*)

No. 3: Secure that sheet! (*To another*) Give a hand at the wheel. Hold her into the wind!

No. 7: Captain, the ship is breaking up!

No. 8 (*on his knees*): O great Chemosh! Save your unworthy servant!

No. 3: This is no time to pray! To work! Lighten ship! Cargo overboard!

> (*The sailors begin throwing imaginary cargo overside, even heavy objects. Ad-lib remarks as, "Give a hand here," "Lift! Lift!" "Take hold there." Let them also take time in the running back and forth to cry out to their gods: "Molech, do not let your servant perish," "Baal! Mercy! Mercy!," "Fair Isis, great Osiris, bear us up!" "Dagon, save us!" When sufficient time is given for all this . . .*)

No. 3: Where is our passenger?

No. 8: Still below, sir! Shall I get him?

No. 3: No! Keep at that cargo! I'll get him!

> (*He goes to* JONAH, *shakes him hard*) Wake up! Wake up!

JONAH (*startled out of his sleep of exhaustion*): What—what is it?

No. 3 (*angry*): What *is* it? Are you deaf, man? The worst storm we ever saw. The ship is sinking. We call on our gods for aid, and here you sleep! Pray your God to save you. Perhaps our lives will be spared as well. Come!

> (JONAH *joins the others.*)

No. 4 (*anxiously*): Captain!

No. 3: Yes, sailor?

No. 4: The cargo is all overside. It isn't enough. We are lost! Is some god punishing all of us for the sin of one? The men want to cast lots to find the guilty man!

No. 3: Very well, sailor.

> (*The sailors gather, kneeling on the floor,* JONAH *standing behind them, watching. They pretend to cast lots. The lot falls to* JONAH *as the guilty man. The others rise and fall back, looking at* JONAH.)

No. 7: What evil have you done? Your God sends this great storm!

No. 8: Who are you? What is your occupation?

No. 4: Where did you come from? Your country?

JONAH (*confessing*): I am Jonah, a prophet of the Lord, God of heaven, Creator of all. He it is I fear and worship.

No. 8: You brought this on us!

No. 7: What is your sin against your God?

JONAH (*miserably*): I am running away. I am afraid of the Lord—I disobeyed him!

No. 8: This great storm is your fault!

No. 7: We don't want to die because of you! What can we do?

JONAH (*miserably*): Cast me overboard. Then the storm will cease.

No. 3: Cargo overboard is one thing—but a man? That's murder. Let us try once more to save our ship. We do not want the blood of this man on our hands.

(*All freeze in place.* No. 5 *comes downstage to speak to the audience.*)

No. 5: They tried. But the storm continued its fury. Finally, seeing that nothing else would save them, they decided to put Jonah overside. First they prayed to the God of Jonah, asking not to be blamed for shedding Jonah's blood. With that, they cast him into the sea.

(*The storm sounds cease.* JONAH *goes upstage left and closes. All* STORYTELLERS *resume first position.*)

STORYTELLERS: Jonah's God ended the storm. Also, he did not forget his prophet. God prepared a great fish to swallow Jonah when he was cast into the raging sea.

No. 1 (*to someone in the audience*): Now don't look so un-believing. Great fish *have* swallowed other live things, and *they* survived!

No. 2: A little the worse for wear!

No. 7 (*with gusto*): All those digestive juices, you know!

Nos. 3,4,8 (*to* 7): Hush! You'll make the girls sick.

No. 7 (*blithely*): Think of poor old Jonah inside that thing three days and nights.

> (JONAH *turns and crouches down.*)

JONAH: Oh, Lord, forgive me! (*Feels his arms and legs.*) I'm alive, I think—wherever I am. (*Looks around.*) Lord, get me out of here! I'll do whatever you say . . . . Lord, I beg you to hear your servant. . . . Forgive me!

STORYTELLERS: So the Lord spoke to the fish, and it vomited Jonah upon dry land.

> (JONAH *stands.* No. 7 *moves toward audience, mischievously.*)

No. 7: The *land* was dry. But Jonah was all wet!

> (*Two of the* STORYTELLERS *pull him back into the group.*)

STORYTELLERS: And the word of the Lord came to Jonah a second time. Jo-o-onah! . . . Jonah!

JONAH (*meekly*): Yes, Lord.

STORYTELLERS: Have you had enough?

JONAH: Yes, Lord!

STORYTELLERS: Jonah, go to Nineveh. Cry out in the streets my words.

JONAH (*bowing his head*): Yes, Lord.

(JONAH *waits a moment, then goes off right. When he is gone—*)

STORYTELLERS: So Jonah crossed the miles
Of the great and hostile land
Between the Great Sea
And the walls of Nineveh,
Capital of Assyria,
A great and wicked city!
The man who said no to God
Came to tell these people
The message of the Lord!

(*The* STORYTELLERS *scatter. No. 1 goes upstage center back, pretends to be a shopkeeper in a booth on the city street. No. 2 goes off right, later to return as a basketmaker bringing wares to the city. No. 3 is a soldier, standing on the street at left, watching the people. Nos. 5,6 are women shoppers at booth of No. 1. No. 4 is the king, 7 and 8 are his servants. These three go off left to wait for their cues. Pretend crowds are on the street. As action begins, No. 1 is trying to sell an imaginary length of cloth to 5 and 6.*)

No. 1: Miladies, feel this! The finest silk I have. The finest in seven moons.

No. 5: The price is too high.

No. 1 (*overdramatically*): Too high! I call heaven to witness! This silk came from the kingdom of the dreaded Khan! Smuggled out over the mountains that touch the sky! Months of travel—to place it in your fair hands. See its beauty? Feel its softness?

No. 6: Yes, yes. It is beautiful, but the price is still too dear. My husband would beat me—

(*Her speech is drowned out by the shouting of the basketmaker, No. 2, who enters right.*)

No. 2 (*calling*): Baskets! . . . Baskets! . . . Pretty baskets!

Who'll buy my baskets! (*Stops by the imaginary shop.*) Will the fine ladies look at my baskets?

No. 1 (*shouting angrily*): Go along! Can't you see these are my customers?

No. 2: Ah, my friend, of course. Let them buy baskets in which to carry your beautiful cloth. (*To No. 6.*) Madam, have you ever seen such workmanship as in this fine basket?

No. 6: It's nice.

> (*Offstage* JONAH *begins calling out, overlapping No. 2's next line.*)

JONAH: Hear me, O people of Nineveh! Listen to the words of the Most High God! Turn away from your evil ways. Listen to the words I say! (*Repeat ad lib as needed.*)

No. 2 (*at the same time*): Nice? Milady, this is poetry in straw, a veritable work of art.

No. 1 (*under* JONAH's *shouting*): Look you here, ladies. Never will you see finer cloth.

No. 5: If it were of purest gold, I still cannot. Who is shouting?

No. 1 (*peering right*): A wandering holy man.

No. 2 (*also looking*): A prophet, milady.

> (JONAH *enters, still calling out.*)

JONAH: Listen to my words, O people of Nineveh. In forty days this great city shall be destroyed! Brick on brick, wall on wall. So sayeth the Lord!

No. 1: Go away with your shouting! We have business here.

JONAH (*looking up*): You see, Lord? I knew all the time they wouldn't listen. (*He shrugs and begins calling again.*) The word of the God of all creation: prepare for the end!

> (JONAH *moves left a few feet. No. 2 follows him, fascinated.*)

JONAH: Hear me, O you who live in doomed Nineveh! I, Jonah, prophet of God, bring you his words.

> (JONAH *keeps on shouting as he walks back and forth. Ad-lib along the things he has said already. Avoid exact repetition.*)

No. 1 (*over* JONAH): The material, ladies!

No. 5: Who can think of cloth with that going on?

No. 6 (*pointing down the street*): There's a soldier. He's looking this way. Shopkeeper, go get him.

> (No. 1 *brings back* No. 3.)

No. 2 (*to* JONAH): Better run! He's trouble.

No. 3 (*to* JONAH): Here, here! What's the fuss? Look, mate, at the crowd you're attracting. You're interfering with business. Go along with you, now.

> (Nos. 7 *and* 8 *enter left and watch.*)

JONAH: I am God's prophet. I come to foretell the end of Nineveh.

No. 6: Officer, this man is crazy.

No. 5: Will you have to arrest him?

No. 3: Oh, I don't know as he's done so much. Just noisy. Now, if he'll quiet down—

JONAH: I must cry out to all Nineveh, a doomed city. So says the Lord, the God of all!

No. 1 (*angrily*): He spoiled a sale for me!

No. 2 (*gleefully*): He's a hero! Rescued two of this crook's victims!

No. 3 (*to* No. 1): I know your sharp dealings, chum. More likely these ladies should thank this man.

No. 1 (*angrily*): Here, now! I'll speak to your captain!

No. 3: You just do that, chum! I'll have a few remarks myself.

No. 5 (*to* 6): Let's leave. Look at all the crowd gathering. My husband will have a fit.

> (*The two friends leave right.*)

No. 1: See? He's running off my customers.

No. 3 (*to* JONAH): What will I do with you, mate?

JONAH (*calling out toward audience, an imaginary crowd*): Listen to me, people of Nineveh! For your sins, Nineveh will fall. Forty days. So speaks the Lord.

No. 3: Here! Stop that. You're getting them all worked up. (Nos. 7 *and* 8 *run to* No. 3)

No. 7: Soldier, take him to the king!

No. 3 (*surprised*): The king?

No. 8: We are the king's servants. Let us take him to our master.

> (*All freeze in the pose a moment. Then all the* STORY-TELLERS *except* No. 4 *resume their first positions.* JONAH *goes upstage, closes.*)

STORYTELLERS: Along the streets to the palace, Jonah kept on crying out God's message.

No. 5: To the crowds lining the way.

No. 6: The people heard his words. They believed the prophet.

STORYTELLERS: Then Jonah came before the king.

No. 1: Jonah told the king what God had said—

No. 2: — recounting his terrible adventures from the beginning.

STORYTELLERS: The king believed Jonah's words, too.

No. 3: The people covered themselves with sackcloth and ashes.

No. 5: The king, too, covered himself with sackcloth and ashes.

STORYTELLERS: Symbols of sorrow and remorse.

No. 7: And the king made a proclamation throughout great Nineveh.

> (*No. 4, as the king, enters. He comes center, opens an imaginary scroll, and "reads."*)

No. 4: By decree of the king—

> Because of the word of the Lord, God of all creation, By his prophet, Jonah.

> Let there be a great fasting. Let not man nor beast eat anything.

> Let them wear sackcloth and ashes for the great sins of Nineveh. Let everyone turn from his wickedness and the violence he showed to others.

> Let us pray the great God will see and will revoke the sentence of doom. Let us pray we perish not by his fierce anger.

> So proclaims the king in great doomed Nineveh!

> > (*The "king" goes to upstage center, closes.*)

STORYTELLERS (*except* No. 4): God . . . heard . . . Nineveh. God . . . saw . . . their . . . repentance. And God . . . revoked the doom . . . upon Nineveh. Merciful is the Lord!

> (*JONAH comes center front as No. 4 rejoins the* STORY-TELLERS.)

STORYTELLERS: Now Jonah was displeased.

No. 1 (*to others*): What he was—was just plain mad!

JONAH (*looking up angrily*): Lord, I knew all the time you wouldn't destroy Nineveh! I knew you'd let them off. I told you so.

STORYTELLERS: Jonah, are you complaining because I spared Nineveh?

JONAH: Look what I went through. I nearly died in that storm.

Then that fish . . . the terrible journey . . . all for nothing because you let them off!

STORYTELLERS: Do you have a right to be angry?

JONAH: Yes, Lord! The worst is what a fool I made of myself: shouting in the streets, involving everyone from the king on down, and then nothing happened. But we know they are the same people. I know they won't hold out. I won't give up hope.

(JONAH *goes downstage left, sits on floor, "pouting."*)

STORYTELLERS: So Jonah went out east of the city, found a scanty bit of shade, made a booth, and sat down to watch Nineveh. The hours passed. The sun was strong and hot. His scanty shade did not protect him.

(Nos. 7 *and* 8 *go behind* JONAH.)

No. 7 (*gleefully*): Here's where I play a gourd vine!

No. 8: And I a cutworm.

STORYTELLERS (*except 7 and 8*): And the Lord let a gourd vine grow to shade Jonah from the hot sun.

(No. 7, *behind* JONAH, *crouches, then rises and stretches out his arms over* JONAH'S *head.*)

JONAH: What a relief. That sun is hot.

STORYTELLERS: Jonah liked his gourd vine. But the next morning God sent a cutworm—

(No. 8 *stands, reaches out and lifts* No. 7's *arms from over* JONAH, *and pulls him back to rejoin the* STORY-TELLERS.)

—and the cutworm injured the gourd vine so that it withered away.

No. 6: Then the sun rose again.

No. 5: And a hot east wind.

STORYTELLERS: After a while, Jonah fainted from the heat.

(JONAH *falls over, holds for a moment, then struggles to his feet.*)

JONAH: I'm so miserable. I wish I could die.

STORYTELLERS: And God said, Jo–o–onah! . . . Jonah! Do you believe you have a right to be angry about the gourd vine?

JONAH: I do!

STORYTELLERS: It was my vine. I put it there.

JONAH (*angrily*): If you treat me this way I might as well die! Why did you take away the gourd vine? It was good for me. It wasn't hurting anything. But you destroyed it!

STORYTELLERS: Jonah, Jonah. Don't you understand? Here you are feeling sorry for a gourd vine. But you didn't feel like that about a great city. You would have me destroy a hundred and twenty thousand people who didn't know right from wrong? Why, Jonah?

(JONAH *closes and freezes. The* STORYTELLERS *look at* JONAH *a moment, then come center, concealing him, except* No. 1.)

STORYTELLERS (*except* 1): Well, that's our story.

No. 1 (*puzzled, joining them*): Wait. What was the ending?

STORYTELLERS: Oh, it is still going on. Again and again. People running away from God. A lot of us are Jonah. We are still working on the problem.

No. 1: Will we find the ending?

STORYTELLERS: Who knows? (*Indicating audience*) Ask *them.*

Questions for Talking

1. How did you like this way of doing a play?

2. Did you mind the same people playing different parts?

3. What did you think of Jonah? Why do you suppose God picked him for such a mission?

4. Did Jonah act in what we call a "childish" manner?

5. Do you ever see grown-ups act "childish"?

6. Do you ever act "childish"?

7. What did the play say to you?

6

Star Light, Star Bright

If you haven't read the Foreword for helpful suggestions, do so now. Playing time is 12 to 15 minutes. Scripture basis is the combined story of the nativity. The cast will wear ordinary clothing. Props needed are a set of supposed play scripts, marked with their names, a table at right back containing a blue scarf for Mary, a brown headdress for Joseph, a white turban for the innkeeper, three sets of small cardboard wings for the angels, and three short capes for the shepherds (a large square of cloth with a hole in the center for the head to go through). Also needed are two stools or boxes and a large cardboard star covered with glitter.

CAST: MRS. WARD, *the adult director of the play;* HANK, *first shepherd;* SMITTY, *second shepherd;* ROB, *third shepherd;* SHELLY, *first angel;* MARGE, *second angel;* BETH, *third angel;* TED, *innkeeper;* LANE, *Joseph;* SUE, *Mary.*

> (MRS. WARD *enters left, scripts in hand. She goes to prop table and checks over props. In a few seconds,* BETH *and* SUE *enter right.*)

MRS. WARD: Hello, Beth, Sue. Glad to see you. You are the first ones to arrive.

BETH: Are we on time?

MRS. WARD: You are indeed. I hope the others come soon.

SUE: We saw some of them just behind us, Mrs. Ward.

MRS. WARD: Good, here they are. (HANK, SMITTY, *and* LANE *enter right.*) Hello, boys. Come in.

HANK: Hi, everybody. You can start now. The important ones are here.

SUE: Also the most humble.

SMITTY: I noticed that, too. Didn't you notice that, Lane?

LANE: Yeah, I noticed it.

> (ROB, SHELLY, MARGE *enter right, running.*)

MARGE: Are we late?

MRS. WARD: Not at all.

SHELLY: Have we missed anything?

BETH: Just one of Hank's modest statements.

SUE: (*at the same time*): Not a thing!

MRS. WARD: You are all on time—

ROB (*interrupting*): Except Ted.

> (TED *enters right.*)

TED: Even, Ted. Hi, all.

ROB: Late, late, Ted is late!

MRS. WARD: No, you aren't, Ted. The first rehearsal begins on time. I'm proud of you.

TED: Don't be too glad, Mrs. Ward. You may have to forgive us another time.

MRS. WARD: Then I will. Sit down somewhere, everyone. (*They do.*) Here are your scripts with the parts marked. (*She gives them out as she calls the names.*) Hank, you are first shepherd. Smitty, you are second shepherd and Rob, third shepherd.

ROB: I'm allergic to wool.

LANE: Are you trying to be one of the angels?

MRS. WARD: Shelly is first angel—

SHELLY (*with exaggerated modesty*): Typecasting, of course.

SMITTY: I noticed that. Didn't you notice that, Lane?

LANE: Yeah, I noticed that.

SHELLY (*with exaggerated kindness*): Mere humans with their little minds. We angels rise above you.

TED (*groaning*): Oh, no!

MRS. WARD: Marge is second angel and Beth, third angel. Sue is Mary, Lane is Joseph, and Ted is the innkeeper.

TED: I run the Bethlehem Holiday Inn. I give special rates to actors.

SUE: I'll take a room.

TED: Sorry, we are full.

SUE: You just said you gave special rates to actors—but you are full.

TED: That's why I can give special rates.

MRS. WARD: Now, let's stop playing. As you know, we plan to do our play just before Christmas. If you'll all work hard, we'll be ready by then. I hope!

LANE: Christmas is a long time off.

MRS. WARD: Not when you are getting a play ready. You'll be surprised at how fast the time will go.

LANE: Okay, let's get at it.

MRS. WARD: Tonight, we'll just look at playing areas and talk about the play and the characters.

ROB: That's not much.

MRS. WARD: Tuesday after school, we'll have a complete read-through.

BETH: Why can't we read it tonight?

SMITTY: Yeah. I can read as good tonight as Tuesday.

BETH (*correcting him*): You can read as *well*.

SMITTY: See? Beth thinks so, too!

ROB: What you really mean is that you'll be as *bad*, Tuesday.

SMITTY: Is that any way to treat a fellow shepherd, I ask you?

MRS. WARD: We won't have time to read it through tonight. Please look at your scripts. Where does the play begin?

HANK: On page 1.

SUE: Oh, dear! Hank, it says the play begins out on a hill near Bethlehem.

MRS. WARD (*hastily*): Let's pretend this whole space is our stage. (*Pointing left*) *That* is the hill where the shepherds are. . . . Oh, dear, I forgot something. Over on that table are some props to make you feel more in character. Will you go put them on? (*They go as she continues*) The blue scarf is for Mary, the brown headdress for Joseph, the turban for Ted. You'll see.

> (*They help each other get ready, ad-libbing remarks in the process.*)

MRS. WARD: All ready, now? Shepherds, go to the hill. Innkeeper, let's pretend your inn is over there (*points stage right*) at the right.

TED (*puzzled, because she seems to be pointing left*): Right? What do you mean, right?

MRS. WARD: At stage right. That is the actor's right, Ted.

> (*TED and the shepherds assume places.*)

HANK: What do we do? Just stand here?

SMITTY: I'm not. I'm a sit-down shepherd. (*He sits.*)

ROB: What's that?

SMITTY: The opposite of a stand-up shepherd, dope!

ROB: Oh. (*He sits.*)

HANK: Well, if you guys sit down, I will, too. (*Sits.*)

MRS. WARD: Dear, no!

HANK: Why not?

MRS. WARD: It doesn't look good.

HANK: Who cares? Those shepherds didn't have an audience.

MRS. WARD: You will, I hope. Up, Hank.

HANK (*groaning*): Okay. After a hard day chasing sheep—

> (*The girls giggle as he drags himself up.*)

MRS. WARD: Lane, you and Sue go off to the left, offstage. Your left, I mean. (*They do.*) Angels, go to the wall there in the center and turn your backs to the audience.

SHELLY (*surprised*): Our *backs*? Why? Won't that look silly?

MRS. WARD: No, Shelly. This just tells the audience you aren't there yet.

MARGE: But we *are* there.

BETH (*patiently*): Not really. (*With a dramatic wave of her hand upward*) We're in heaven!

MARGE: *You* may be in heaven. *I'm* at the back of the stage with my face to the wall. (*All angels close.*)

MRS. WARD: Thank you, girls—I think. Now, Ted, you turn your back also.

TED: I'm inside the inn. Right?

MRS. WARD: Right. Now, everybody, look at your scripts. The play opens with the shepherds talking about the bright star in the sky.

SUE (*calling from off left*): Where's the star?

MRS. WARD: Lane, please look on the prop table. (LANE *finds the star, holds it up.*) We'll have to think of some way to hold it up.

LANE (*brightly*): How about a fishing pole in the baptistry? Or from over the front balcony?

BETH: That's silly. It would bobble.

ROB (*bragging*): Not with a *boy* holding it.

SHELLY: Want to bet?

MRS. WARD (*quickly*): Look at the script. The shepherds are on the hill.

HANK: They see the star.

SMITTY: It's a star. It's a bird! It's Supershepherd!

MRS. WARD: Look at your scripts, please, cast! Turn to page 3 where the angels enter.

MARGE (*reading*): Oh, oh! It says we enter singing! You just lost an angel. Mrs. Ward, I can't carry a tune.

TED (*with feeling*): She sure can't!

SMITTY (*scornfully*): Look who's talking—"Old Squeaker."

MRS. WARD (*firmly*): The Carol Choir will sing from the balcony. Now, then, the angels come to the shepherds. Do it, girls!

BETH: Now?

SMITTY: Now, she said. Come on, you angels. (*The girls go to the shepherds.*) Mrs. Ward, I have an idea! Let's have them *fly* in.

MRS. WARD: Never mind. Look down those pages. See, girls? You tell the shepherds about the baby and the star—

LANE (*off*): On a fishing pole! (*all giggle*)

MRS. WARD: And right on to page 6 at the top where you shepherds go to Bethlehem. Then the spotlight goes off.

HANK: What spotlight?

MRS. WARD: Didn't I say?

HANK: No, you didn't.

MRS. WARD: Sorry. Well, there will be a spotlight on the scene—the one that is happening—all through the play.

SUE (*off*): A real spotlight?

MRS. WARD: Actually just a slide projector. But it makes a good spotlight.

> (*At this point, the room light goes off, and the spotlight falls on* TED *at the inn. He turns to the audience. He is the innkeeper, now.* SUE *and* LANE, *as Mary and Joseph, walk slowly into the light,* JOSEPH *helping* MARY.)

JOSEPH: Innkeeper! Innkeeper!

INNKEEPER (*firmly*): No, don't ask. It's no use.

JOSEPH: But sir, I need—

INNKEEPER: I know. I simply cannot help you.

JOSEPH: But my wife is very tired.

INNKEEPER: There's nothing left. Not a corner. Nothing.

JOSEPH: We've come a long way. From Nazareth.

INNKEEPER: Too bad. That's not my problem.

JOSEPH: The baby is due soon.

INNKEEPER (*sharply*): Why didn't you leave your wife at home? Wherever you said that is.

JOSEPH: Nazareth.

INNKEEPER: Well—wherever. Very foolish.

MARY (*wearily*): I wanted Joseph near when— But you are right, sir, it is not your concern.

INNKEEPER: That's a sensible girl.

MARY: Before we go on, may I rest on your doorstep a moment, sir? I am so tired.

INNKEEPER (*grudgingly*): I guess so. But mind you don't stay long. Makes the place look bad, people draped all over the front.

(MARY *sits on a stool and leans against* JOSEPH. *The* INNKEEPER *watches them a moment, then he speaks.*)

INNKEEPER: Listen! It's not much—just a stable for the beasts. But it's fairly clean and not too cold, built the way it is in that hillside. It's around back. If you have no place else you could stay there tonight.

MARY (*gratefully*): Oh, Joseph, yes!

JOSEPH: Thank you, Innkeeper. I'm sure it will do quite well. Come, Mary. (*He helps her up. The* INNKEEPER *picks up her stool and a second stool and moves them a little farther right. The spotlight follows.*)

INNKEEPER: Here it is. Maybe I could find some extra blankets against the cold.

JOSEPH (*as he helps Mary sit*): We have enough. Thank you, sir.

INNKEEPER (*exiting right*): Good night, then.

JOSEPH: Good night, sir.

(*The spotlight leaves them and goes to the shepherds and angels who are posed as we last saw them, except that now they are the* ANGELS *and* SHEPHERDS. *First shepherd is standing, and the other two are kneeling. The angels are near.*)

FIRST SHEPHERD (*still frightened at the sight of angels*): To—to Bethlehem? We—we must go to Bethlehem?

FIRST ANGEL: Find the stable behind the inn. There you will see the child—just as we have said.

SECOND ANGEL: Glory to God in the highest! Glory to God!

THIRD ANGEL: Peace to men on earth! Peace.

> (*The* ANGELS *step back out of the light and quietly move over to the inn. They stand behind* MARY *and* JOSEPH.)

SECOND SHEPHERD (*stands*): Were they real? Or did we dream?

FIRST SHEPHERD: How could we all dream the same dream?

THIRD SHEPHERD: If we go see, we'll know if it was a dream. Come on!

> (*They walk slowly right and stop at the inn where the light can encompass them all.* TED *will be the only absent one.* MARY *and* JOSEPH *are seated, and* MARY *has her arms cradled as if holding a baby.*)

MARY: Good morning, shepherds! Come in. You are welcome.

THIRD SHEPHERD (*kneeling*): It is true. All of it is true.

SECOND SHEPHERD (*kneeling*): The child as they said.

FIRST SHEPHERD: Heavenly voices told us to come see the child. All is as they said.

MARY (*looking at child*): Here he is. Did you ever see a more beautiful child?

SECOND SHEPHERD (*looking*): Never.

THIRD SHEPHERD: It *is* all like a dream. The voices. Now the child. To think we should see him. The gift of God.

> (*Suddenly the spotlight goes out. In the darkness,* MRS. WARD *speaks.*)

MRS. WARD: Ted? Get the room lights. (*The room lights come on.*) Oh, dear, we'll have to do something about that light. Can't have this happening during the performance.

> (*None of the cast has moved. Now, slowly, they all*

move quietly away from SUE, *who remains on the stool, her arms still cradled.*)

MRS. WARD: I'm sorry about the light. At least now you see how the play goes. Before Tuesday, why don't you try to learn as many of your lines as pos—Sue! You can get up now. We are through for tonight.

SUE (*softly, not moving*): What if it were tonight?

LANE (*going to her*): What if what were tonight?

SUE (*stands, lets her arms down slowly*): Jesus— What if he were being born tonight instead of then. Do you think anyone would see the star? Would there be a room for him?

LANE: Maybe.

TED (*joining them*): Maybe not. They were awfully poor, weren't they? Mary and Joseph, I mean. Holiday Inns cost money. They don't give rooms away. That's business.

BETH (*joining them*): Where would they go, then? Now, I mean. Poor people.

ROB (*returning*): If they were *that* poor . . . How would it feel to have *no* place you could go?

SHELLY: Because you were poor?

MARGE: Or because your town—or your whole country—was gone. Like war.

SMITTY: I've seen the news pictures.

SHELLY (*bursting out*): Oh, I wish the *whole world* was *good!*

BETH: With room enough for everybody!

MARGE: And food enough!

MRS. WARD (*softly*): And love enough?

(*They all look at each other a silent moment, thinking, wishing.*)

That's really what our play is all about, isn't it?

HANK: Love. Yeah.

MRS. WARD: The great big wonderful marvelous love of God. That's all for tonight, cast. Thank you for coming.

SUE (*earnestly*): Mrs. Ward, I'll know all my lines by Tuesday! I will! (*All agree, each in his or her own words.*)

MRS. WARD: Thank you for trying. Good night. See you Tuesday.

(*She watches them leave, looking after them a moment. She bows her head. Then she looks up.*) Thank you, Father. Thank you.

Questions for Talking

1. Were you ever in a play? Did you like being someone else?

2. In the play, did the boys and girls sound like those you know? Why did they tease each other?

3. What does the play say to you? What is the main point?

4. Did you like the play? Tell why, either way.

7

In a Mustard Seed

If you haven't read the Foreword for helpful suggestions, do so now. Playing time is 12 to 15 minutes. Scripture basis: Luke 9:28–42; Mark. 9:9–29; Matt. 17:14–21. Let someone report on the superstitions that once surrounded epilepsy. Names not in the Bible given to characters are ASA *for the father and* REUBEN *for the unfortunate son.*

Players may wear biblical costumes or ordinary clothing. You will need a stretcher: two poles with cloth stretched around and secured, a blanket or sheet.

Always in a play about Jesus there is the question whether to have him seen or not. Although in this play it is possible to use a real character, the play is designed so that he may remain unseen. With a microphone the lines may be spoken from anywhere. Without a mike, a screen at right may hide the actor. In either case, the other actors simply pretend he is where he's supposed to be, reacting as expected.

CAST: ANDREW, *a disciple of Jesus;* MATTHEW, *another disciple;* ASA, *the father;* REUBEN, *the son;* PETER, JAMES, *and* JOHN, *other disciples;* VOICE OF JESUS; *the* CROWD, *as many as desired. Note that* CROWD 1, CROWD 2, *etc., means these actors. The parts may be combined or redistributed to stretch to a larger* CROWD.

(MATTHEW *and* ANDREW *enter left, followed by the* CROWD.)

MATTHEW (*turning on them*): There's no use your following us! Jesus isn't here.

CROWD 1: Where is he? Where can we find him?

MATTHEW: I don't know exactly. He went off with John, James, and Peter.

CROWD 1: When will he return?

ANDREW: We don't know. Soon, we hope.

CROWD 2: You are his disciples. You help us.

ANDREW: How can we help you?

CROWD 2 (*holding out his hand, twisted into a fist*): My hand— see? It is crippled. You can heal it?

MATTHEW (*hesitating*): Well, Jesus usually—

CROWD 3 (*disgusted*): Aw, come away. They can't do anything for you.

MATTHEW (*aroused*): Perhaps we can! Come here.

> (CROWD 2 *comes to* MATTHEW, *frightened now. The whole* CROWD *comes closer.*)

MATTHEW (*with authority*): Hold out your hand! (CROWD 2 *slowly extends twisted hand.*) In the name of God, the Father, straighten your fingers! (*Slowly* CROWD 2 *straightens out fingers, flexing them. Turns to others and waves hand, then runs from one to another, touching them and showing his hand.* Be creative in demonstration.)

CROWD 2: Look! Look! My fingers! See? They work like anyone's! Like yours! And yours! Praise be to God! My hand—I can use it again! I can work again!

> (*Others have been rejoicing, ad-libbing remarks to and about him. Meanwhile* MATTHEW *and* ANDREW *withdraw to stage front and speak over the noise.*)

MATTHEW: It *worked.* Something happened to me. It *worked,* Andrew.

ANDREW: Then we can heal, too. Not only the Master, but we, too, can heal, Matthew.

> (*In a moment,* CROWD 2's *joy is controlled. All gather again around* MATTHEW *and* ANDREW. ASA *pushes through the* CROWD. REUBEN *remains upstage behind* CROWD.)

ASA: Sirs! Honored sirs!

MATTHEW (*turning*): You speak to us?

ASA (*bowing low*): Honored sirs, you are disciples of the Nazarene prophet, are you not?

MATTHEW: We are.

ASA: Did you not cure the twisted hand of that man?

MATTHEW: Well—yes, you could say so.

ASA (*kneeling*): Sirs, I beg you to cure my son! My only son, sirs.

> (*Suddenly, from behind the* CROWD, REUBEN *is heard to groan loudly. Then he falls to the floor and cries and groans. The* CROWD *turns around to look at the boy on the floor, concealing him from the audience, which can only hear him. While he is suffering the "seizure," the* CROWD *stifles cries and murmurs of pity, with much noise, all talking at once.*)

CROWD 3: He's having a fit!

CROWD 4: Look, look!

CROWD 5: A demon possesses him!

CROWD 6: He will hurt himself, the poor boy.

CROWD 7: What's the matter? What is it?

CROWD 2: He has a devil! A devil dwells inside!

CROWD 1: Somebody hold him. He will harm himself!

ASA (*he has pushed through the* CROWD): Reuben! Reuben! Let me through!

> (*The noise subsides. The* CROWD *parts.* REUBEN *is on the floor, eyes closed, unmoving.* ASA *kneels beside him, upstage, rubbing his limp hand and wiping his face.*)

ASA: Reuben, my son. Your father is here.

ANDREW: What is it?

ASA: This is my son, of whom I spoke. He has these—seizures. Now he will lie like a log for a time, and when he wakens, he will remember nothing.

CROWD 5: A demon possesses him, I say.

CROWD 4: His father should shut him up somewhere.

CROWD 7: That's right. He's a danger.

CROWD 6: Only to himself. Perhaps the Nazarene— (*remembering, to* MATTHEW *and* ANDREW) Can *you* cure this boy?

ANDREW: I don't know.

MATTHEW (*doubtfully*): If we can open a hand, can we not cure a whole body?

ASA (*at their side*): Oh, sirs, I shall be grateful! He is a good boy.

MATTHEW: How long has he been possessed by this demon?

ASA: Since a baby. Often he has fallen in the fire and several times in the river when the demon groans within him. He bears scars and bruises. Oh, sirs, cure my son, I pray!

ANDREW (*at center front*): Bring him over here, out of the crowd.

ASA (*pointing right, to some of* CROWD): Go to that house and bring a litter, please. Just inside the door. (*To disciples*) It is always ready for we know not when the demon will possess him.

> (*Four of* CROWD *get litter, or stretcher, off right, roll* REUBEN *onto it. Then they bring him center front.*)

ASA (*to disciples during above action*): Reuben is my only son. I am Asa, a cloth merchant. Whatever the fee is, I'll gladly pay.

ANDREW: There is no fee.

ASA: The physicians and doctors tell me nothing can be done. I fear one day he will fall into the fire, and no one will be near to save him.

MATTHEW: We will do what we can. Now, stand back, everyone.

(*The* CROWD *steps back, forming a semicircle.*)

MATTHEW: Reuben, can you hear me?

CROWD 1: He is like one dead!

MATTHEW (*after pause*): Reuben, your father, Asa, is here.

ASA (*kneeling by* REUBEN, *picking up his hand*): Reuben, do you hear me? Reuben, these men will try to help you.

MATTHEW (*firmly*): Reuben! Reuben! Get up! Demon, come out of him!

(REUBEN *is motionless. The* CROWD *moves restlessly.* ANDREW *takes* MATTHEW's *place.*)

ANDREW: Reuben! Give up the demon that holds you! Get up!

(*Nothing happens. The* CROWD *is even more restless.*)

CROWD 7: He does not move.

CROWD 6: Is he dead?

ASA (*sadly*): He is alive, but is as one asleep.

CROWD 5: The disciples of the Nazarene are helpless!

CROWD 2 (*defensively*): They cured me. Look! They cured me!

CROWD 4: How do we know you were not faking all the time?

CROWD 3: *They* are fakes!

CROWD 1: Drive them out!

CROWD 2: No, no! They cured me truly!

CROWD 7: Seize them. Cast them out!

(*Some of the* CROWD *take hold of* ANDREW *and* MAT-

THEW *and begin pulling them right.* PETER, JAMES, *and*
JOHN run in from right.)

PETER: Andrew! Matthew! What is wrong?

(JAMES *and* JOHN *rescue* MATTHEW *and* ANDREW *from
the* CROWD.)

JAMES: Let them go!

JOHN: What are you doing?

(*The* CROWD *drops back, faced with these reinforce-
ments. Now is the time for Jesus' involvement. If he is
actually there, he will enter right, and the whole group
will turn so he is the point of focus. If only his voice is
heard, all will turn as if he is standing right front at
the edge of the stage.*)

JESUS: Peace! What is the trouble?

(*The* CROWD *say to each other such things as:* "*The
Nazarene,*" "*It is the prophet,*" "*This is the man,*" "*The
healer.*")

JESUS: Matthew, Andrew, what is the matter?

MATTHEW: We—failed, Lord.

JESUS: Failed?

ANDREW: Not completely. (*Pulls cured man forward.*) Lord,
we made this man's hand whole and well again.

CROWD 2 (*holding up hand for all to see*): It's true. Always it
has been a lump. Now my fingers move like any other man's.

JESUS: That is good. Is that all?

MATTHEW: We failed with this man's son, Lord.

ASA (*bowing low toward Jesus*): Rabbi, this boy is my only
son. He is possessed of a demon that makes him thresh
about and groan and gnash his teeth. Then he falls into
a sleep and does not know what has happened. He is in
danger of death when the demon moves within him.

CROWD 1: These men tried to drive out the demon and failed.

JESUS: What did *you* do for the boy?

CROWD 1 (*startled*): Who, me? Nothing, Master, nothing.

JESUS: And the rest of you?

> (*Each* CROWD *ad-libs his innocence of any involvement whatsoever.*)

JESUS: Then if you did nothing, do you have a right to condemn two men who at least tried to help?

CROWD 1: But they *failed.*

JESUS: Human beings often fail. That is why God must forgive them.

ASA (*turning away*): Then my son is doomed to die.

JESUS: I did not say this.

ASA (*to Jesus, hopefully*): Lord, can you help my son? Lord?

> (*Silence as the* CROWD *draws back to watch the litter.*)

JESUS (*after pause*): Oh, faithless and perverse generation! How long shall I bear with you? Bring the boy to me.

> (*Four in the* CROWD *nervously carry the litter stage right front. They quickly move back. Suddenly* REUBEN *begins to groan again and roll his head back and forth, with wildly threshing arms. He kicks and twists violently. The* CROWD *reacts with cries about the demon, as before. Be very serious to avoid laughter.* ASA *tries to hold the boy still but can't. The five disciples stand by helplessly. Jesus speaks.*)

JESUS: Reuben, hold still! (*A few movements, then he is still as before.*)

ASA: You see, my Lord? Your disciples could do nothing for my son.

JESUS (*with compassion*): I see, Asa. Reuben, hear me.

(*One hand moves. The* CROWD *reacts with whispers.*)

JESUS: Reuben, there is a sickness in you. From this moment, that sickness is gone forever. Rise up, Reuben!

(REUBEN *opens his eyes. Then slowly he sits up. The* CROWD *reacts.*)

ASA (*kneeling beside his son*): My son! Do you know me?

REUBEN (*puzzled*): Of course, Father.

ASA: How do you feel, my son?

(*If an actor is seen as* JESUS, *he will reach out to* REU-BEN *and help him up. If only a* VOICE, ASA *will help the boy stand.*)

REUBEN (*bewildered*): Fine, Father. I've never felt so well. What's happened, Father?

ASA: Praise be to God! The Galilean has made you well! (*To the* CROWD) Look at my son! He is whole, like any other boy!

(*He ad-libs in this vein, and the* CROWD *responds individually, all rejoicing in the recovery of the boy. After a moment,* ASA *turns back to Jesus.*)

ASA: How can I thank you, Lord? What can I do to repay this great favor?

JESUS: Nothing, Asa. Your joy and your faith are pay enough. Go, now. Rejoice in your son.

ASA: Yes, yes. (*To the* CROWD) Come to my house. We shall have a feast of celebration. My son is whole again! (*He turns back to* JESUS.) Lord, will you honor my house?

JESUS: Thank you, Asa. But I must be on my way. Farewell.

ASA (*kneeling briefly*): Farewell, Lord. (*Rising, puts arms around* REUBEN. *One of* CROWD *takes along litter, all go right, talking about miracle. When all have gone, the disciples look to Jesus.*)

MATTHEW: I don't understand. We were able to heal the hand. Why could we not restore the boy?

JESUS: You had the faith that the hand would come straight. Then when you faced a greater test, your faith failed.

ANDREW: What could we have done?

JESUS: Found your faith again. Sometimes it comes only by fasting and prayer. With enough faith, we can do anything.

ANDREW: How much is enough?

JESUS: You can begin with faith no larger than a mustard seed, the smallest of seeds. Then through prayer that faith will grow, as the plant grows, until it is almost like a tree. There is always enough faith if we but nurture it. Come, now, let us go into Galilee.

(*All leave right.*)

Questions for Talking

1. In the play, who had faith like a mustard seed?

2. Can you believe in something and then not believe in it?

3. Even if you know you can't help someone, should you try anyway? What good is this?

4. Which character did you like best? Why?

5. Why was the crowd angry when the disciples failed?

8

A Neighbor Is Like Me

If you haven't read the Foreword for helpful suggestions, do so now. Playing time is 13 to 16 minutes. Scripture basis is Luke 10:25–37. In a Bible encyclopedia, look up priest, Levite, *and* Samaritan. *This story concerns perjudice between the Samaritans and Jews, but the truths apply to all prejudice.*

Let the cast dress to show this idea. They may wear masks painted in the colors herein suggested, or use makeup. Each character, except NARRATOR, has a face of a different color. For the colors of makeup, order Stein's Lining Sticks, @ 50¢ each, from Paramount Theatrical Supplies, 32 West 20th Street, New York, N.Y. You will need No. 6 Light Brown, No. 14 Vermilion, No. 16 Yellow, No. 19 Green, No. 15 White, No. 17 Black. Liners are like small sticks of grease paint. DIRECTIONS: apply cold cream to the face and wipe off. Apply the liner and blend on the skin. Add eye and lip accents. Powder generously. Dust powder off. The makeup is "set." To remove, apply cold cream and wipe off.

Costume the cast in the exaggerated styles clowns wear, excepting the NARRATOR again. Invent your own. Here are some suggestions to start you creating.

The MAN: light brown face, torn ragged clothes with poster paint "blood." A "cut" on the head.

The SOLDIER: red face, Napoleon hat of cardboard, mixed military clothing, all too big.

The PRIEST: yellow face, tall, exaggerated cardboard miter, backward collar, narrow, long shawl (a strip of old sheet, dyed red).

The LEVITE: green face, tall hat, big glasses, long, loose coat with a ruler, tablet, and chalk eraser fastened to it.

The SAMARITAN: white face, with thin lines of all the other colors used, a robe covered with long strips of cloth of various colors, brief white headdress similar to that of biblical shepherds.

The INNKEEPER: *black face, old pants and shirt (too big), a long butcher's apron, and a chef's cap.*

NOTE: *in these loose clothes and this face makeup, girls can play boys' parts easily.*

The only staging needed is placing at left two chairs or boxes for the bed.

The lights go off, and the cast gets in place in the darkness. They will be arranged across stage back in an irregular semi-circle, with their backs to the audience (closed). Use natural levels. Add small boxes or platforms if needed for variety.

The lights come on. The cast is seen right to left: the MAN, the SOLDIER, the PRIEST, the LEVITE, the SAMARITAN, the INN-KEEPER. The NARRATOR strolls in through the audience. He stands off center of the playing area.

NARRATOR: There they are. The characters in the play, I mean. You may not like their looks. None of them looks like you. Except me, of course. (*He looks over the audience and smiles.*) Maybe I ought to do something about that. You see, their colors and costumes are symbolic—whatever you want them to be. Our story starts this way: Once when Jesus was in Judea, the usual crowd gathered around. In the crowd was one of those *lawyers.* You remember. Always bugging Jesus.

SOLDIER (*turning, speaking in exaggerated slyness*): Sir! How can I inherit eternal life?

NARRATOR (*annoyed*): You're not the lawyer! You're a Roman soldier, a renegade. Turn around!

SOLDIER (*reasonably*): Have you got a lawyer?

NARRATOR: No.

SOLDIER: Okay, then I'll play the lawyer now, and you can speak *his* lines.

NARRATOR: Well—okay. (*changing tone*) Lawyer, what does the law say? What's written there?

SOLDIER (*coming forward, pretending to read and paraphrasing Scripture from an imaginary scroll*): It says here to love the Lord, your God, with all your heart, soul, and strength, and your neighbor as you love yourself.

NARRATOR: That's it then. Go and do what it says.

SOLDIER: Well, now, I have to think this one over. Just who *is* my neighbor that I'm supposed to love so much?

MAN (*turning*): I come in here.

SOLDIER: Not yet! Let me get set! (*Returns to his place and closes.*)

MAN (*coming forward*): Now, I play a traveling salesman from Jerusalem. I had clients in Jericho, so I was on that road. Oh, I'd been there lots of times before and nothing ever happened. The traffic is sort of heavy, like on highways.

SOLDIER (*turns and joins the MAN*): I was on that road, too. Me and some other guys from the barracks in Jerusalem. You know—that Fortress Antonia. We'd been drinking and living it up over in Jericho. Ran out of money, that's what.

MAN: So you came after mine!

SOLDIER: Yep, we did. The road was sort of empty right then. No witnesses around. You came along all by yourself. One of the guys said, "Let's take him!" We were just drunk enough, I guess. So we did.

MAN: Barbarians!

SOLDIER (*annoyed*): Now, look here, Jew! Who's in control of this country? Who's top dog, huh? Romans, that's who! We don't think it's so much to kill a Jew!

MAN (*ruefully*): As it turned out, I believe you.

SOLDIER (*rubbing his jaw*): You put up quite a tussle.

MAN: Not for long.

SOLDIER: Not against Romans! Anyway, we got out of there with enough for a spree. Thanks, old man.

MAN: Don't mention it.

SOLDIER (*as he turns to resume his first position*): Oh, yeah. I remember we left you in the ditch by the side of the road.

MAN: I *don't* remember. I don't remember anything for quite a while. (*He goes front center and stretches out on the floor.*)

(*The PRIEST turns. His hands are together as if praying.*)

NARRATOR: The next thing we find out is about a priest who came along.

PRIEST (*reprovingly, as he comes forward with dignity*): I didn't just "come along." You make it sound as if I had nothing better to do that day. The fact is I had church business in Jericho. I am a busy man. It was a sacrifice for me to make that trip.

NARRATOR: Well you did come along. Admit it.

PRIEST (*annoyed*): I am not on trial here! Probably several others came along before I did. That was a main road. Why don't you ask them?

NARRATOR: Because the story doesn't mention them. I don't know who they were.

INNKEEPER (*turning but remaining in place*): Ask me. I know who some were. They stopped at my inn later that day, telling about the terrible crime they saw.

NARRATOR: Turn around! You aren't in the story yet!

INNKEEPER: I was in the story when I heard about it from the first one of those travelers who stopped with me.

NARRATOR: Then why wasn't *he* in the story?

INNKEEPER: Not "he." Four altogether. How do I know why they weren't in the story? They all four saw that guy in the ditch, and ran.

MAN (*raising head from floor*): Why?

INNKEEPER: Afraid they'd be next, I guess. All these muggings going on. Those robbers could be hiding out and using that body for bait.

NARRATOR: All right. You had your say. Now wait your turn. Man, back to your ditch!

> (*The* INNKEEPER *shrugs and closes. The* MAN *is still again.*)

PRIEST (*with dignity*): May I go now? I have other duties.

NARRATOR: Wait! The innkeeper said those four didn't stop because they were afraid. What's your excuse? Aren't priests supposed to care about people?

PRIEST: I *do*. *Live* ones. Oh, I saw him over there. I—I thought he was dead.

NARRATOR: But you didn't go check.

PRIEST: Certainly not! He wasn't one of *my* congregation. He wasn't like us at all. You could see that. I have a big responsibility to my *own* people. No time for—riffraff.

NARRATOR: He wasn't riffraff.

PRIEST (*annoyed*): You couldn't tell. Those torn, bloody clothes. No baggage. Besides, his face was—*brown*.

LEVITE (*turning, coming to* PRIEST): I cannot keep silent any longer.

PRIEST: Who are you?

LEVITE: I am the Levite in the story.

PRIEST (*friendlier*): Oh, yes. You came along after I did.

LEVITE: That's true. I agree with you entirely. He *did* look dead. (*To* NARRATOR) This priest was quite justified in going on. Report a dead body or call the police at all and and you are in trouble for weeks! Investigation. Trial.

NARRATOR: Did *you* check?

LEVITE: No. But save your lecture. I admit I made a mistake. I know now he wasn't dead. I was in a hurry to get to Jericho.

NARRATOR: Such a hurry you couldn't stop.

LEVITE: Look! I knew someone would stop soon—someone of his type. I was the main speaker at a convention of educators. How would it look if I were late? Or arrived with some of his blood on me? There *are* standards! I'm glad he made it, but obviously he wasn't my kind—not my responsibility.

PRIEST: I say, why don't we get together sometime? We seem to have some things in common.

LEVITE (*as they go to resume their first positions*): Delighted! Make it soon.

NARRATOR (*to audience*): You see how it was? There the MAN lay, slowly bleeding to death. Nobody helped him because they didn't like his torn clothes, or didn't want to get involved with the police, or thought he didn't count because his face was a different color.

SAMARITAN (*turning, remaining there*): My face isn't his color. I stopped.

NARRATOR: You are the Samaritan, aren't you?

PRIEST (*turning*): Samaritans don't care who they are with!

NARRATOR: It isn't your turn! (*The* PRIEST *closes.*) Now, Samaritan, the story goes that you came along that road, after the priest and the Levite.

SAMARITAN: I was on my way to Jericho for—well, you don't need to know my business.

NARRATOR: It was important?

SAMARITAN: I thought so, or I wouldn't have gone.

88

NARRATOR: As important as a speech? Or church business?

SAMARITAN: To me it was.

NARRATOR: Then you saw the injured man?

SAMARITAN (*moving over to the recumbent* MAN *and carrying out the actions*): I saw him in the ditch. I went over to him. I kneeled down beside him. (*Feels* MAN's *pulse*) His pulse was good, but he was unconscious.

NARRATOR (*in mock distaste*): You—*touched* him? You, a Samaritan, touched a *Jew?*

SAMARITAN (*looking up*): How else can you feel a pulse?

NARRATOR (*joining the two*): But look at him! He's not like you?

SAMARITAN: So what?

NARRATOR (*urgently*): Look here, Samaritan! A priest and a Levite just passed him by. They were Jews. If he were conscious, he'd probably hate you because you are a Samaritan. Why don't you just go on? Stay out of it?

SAMARITAN (*concerned*): Look at him! He'll die if he doesn't get help. I don't care who he is. He's a *man*, isn't he? He's in need, isn't he? Here, give me a hand.

NARRATOR (*drawing back*): Me? I'm not in the story!

SAMARITAN (*grinning*): No, but my donkey was. You can be my donkey.

NARRATOR: Look here. Are you trying to insult me?

SAMARITAN: Oh, it's no insult. My donkey was an excellent beast. He looked different, too, but we got along fine. Take hold.

NARRATOR (*reluctantly helping him get the* MAN *to his feet*): All right. Where are we going?

SAMARITAN: Down the road a piece. There's a good inn there.

NARRATOR: You're taking *him* to an inn? A respectable hotel? What will they think?

SAMARITAN: You needn't worry. The inn has a good stable—for you.

NARRATOR: Very funny. I mean, will they take—him?

SAMARITAN: People like money. Money has no color bar.

(*They put the* MAN's *arms across their shoulders and "walk" him to the left.*)

INNKEEPER (*turning*): Here, what's all this?

SAMARITAN: An injured man. Where can we put him?

INNKEEPER (*with distaste*): He's bloody and dirty!

SAMARITAN: I noticed that, too.

INNKEEPER: Blood ruins things!

SAMARITAN: You'll be paid.

INNKEEPER (*distastefully*): He doesn't look as if he can pay—even if he lives.

SAMARITAN: My good man! *I* will pay. If you'll let me put this man down, I will pay you now.

INNKEEPER (*grudgingly*): Okay. Put him here.

(*They lower him onto the boxes or chairs left.*)

NARRATOR (*to* SAMARITAN): Are you through with me?

SAMARITAN: Yes, thank you. Feel free to use the stable now!

NARRATOR (*returning to his place*): Stable!

INNKEEPER: Now about the pay—

SAMARITAN: Can't you do something for him first?

INNKEEPER: Now look here! You are a Samaritan—

SAMARITAN: I guess it shows.

INNKEEPER: You bet it does! You're a Samaritan and here you come bringing in this— this—

SAMARITAN: *Man*, Sir.

INNKEEPER: Man, then. No telling what he's been up to by the look of him.

SAMARITAN: Or what's been done to him?

INNKEEPER: That's not the point. I don't trust Samaritans. Where's my money?

SAMARITAN (*giving him imaginary money*): Here. Take this. Is that enough?

INNKEEPER: Well—

SAMARITAN: All right, here's more. Is *that* enough?

INNKEEPER: For a while.

SAMARITAN: In two days I'll be back along this road. I'll stop and pay any more that's due. Now are you satisfied?

INNKEEPER: I guess so.

SAMARITAN: Then for heaven's sake, get busy on him. I'm on my way.

INNKEEPER: Wait. Can I ask something?

SAMARITAN: Ask ahead.

INNKEEPER: You puzzle me. You're a Samaritan. Look at you. Then look at him. I'd say he was a Jew. Now, why are you doing this? Do you know him?

SAMARITAN: I never saw him before.

INNKEEPER: Then why?

SAMARITAN: Oh, I don't know. Because he was *there* and in need, I guess.

INNKEEPER: Samaritans! I'll never understand them.

SAMARITAN: Don't try. Life's more interesting that way. Let me ask you something. You let *me* in this hotel, right?

INNKEEPER: Sure.

SAMARITAN: You took my money, and we made a deal. Right?

INNKEEPER: Sure.

SAMARITAN: Well, you're a Jew—and I'm not.

INNKEEPER (*enlightened*): Yeah!

> (*The* INNKEEPER *and* SAMARITAN *go to their places and close.*)

NARRATOR (*to audience*): So that's the story.

MAN (*sitting up, stretching*): Good! Now I can stretch.

> (*All the others turn and come front in a loose grouping, relaxed.*)

SOLDIER: Is it over?

PRIEST: Yeah. Well—see you around.

LEVITE: Let's get this stuff off.

> (PRIEST *and* LEVITE *leave right.*)

INNKEEPER (*to* SOLDIER): If this were real life, I'd have to thank you for bringing me business.

SOLDIER (*as he and* INNKEEPER *leave right*): Say, that's right. Maybe we could go into partnership.

SAMARITAN (*to the* MAN): Looks as if you're left with me again.

> (*They start off right.*)

NARRATOR (*joining them*): And me. I *did* play that donkey well, didn't I!

MAN: Best acting I ever saw. I think it was really YOU!

Questions for Talking

1. Did you like the costumes and makeup (or masks)?
2. Did it take you long to get used to them?
3. Would you like the play better without them?
4. What did the play say to you?
5. Did what is said have anything to do with your life at school?
6. Did the play remind you of any situations you have seen?
7. Were you ever a neighbor to a "neighbor"?

9

A Coin Is Missing

If you haven't read the Foreword for helpful suggestions, do so now. Playing time is 10 to 12 minutes. The Scripture basis is Luke 15: 8–10. This brief play is concerned with suspicion and distrust. It is imaginary, an allegory based on the Scripture, reflecting human nature. The staging is stylized (that is, constricted, formal).

Ruth James
(Neighbors)

Rebecca
(Little Girl)

David
(Little Boy)

Rachel
(Her Friend)
Priscilla
(The Woman)

If there are natural levels present in the acting area, adapt to them. If not enough, add small platforms or levels on which place chairs or tall stools or a combination.

Besides this special staging, special lighting will help this playlet. Create pools of light on each player by small spotlights from above. Make the lights from cans, No. 1½ or medium juice cans. Remove one end, cut a hole in the other for a light socket. Paint the inside with stove black for a sharp, undiffused light. Stove black may be purchased at a hardware store. Do not use any other kind of black paint. (It will continue to smoke and smell badly.) Use a bulb to fit the can, not touching the sides. Suspend over each actor.

Dress in modern clothes. DAVID *and* REBECCA *may wear blue jeans and knit shirts.* REBECCA *is a boyish girl.*

Props need are ten coins for PRISCILLA *and a ball for the children. All other props and the scenery are in the imagination of the beholders.*

CAST: PRISCILLA, *the woman;* RACHEL, *her friend;* RUTH *and* JAMES, *neighbors and friends;* REBECCA, *a little neighbor girl;* DAVID, *a little neighbor boy.*

> (As the play opens, actors take their places, each in his own spotlight, assuming comfortable, meaningful poses. In a moment, PRISCILLA stands, lines up her coins on the seat of her stool or chair, looks at them proudly. Then she turns and calls)

PRISCILLA (*calling*): Rachel! Rachel, are you home? Yoo-hoo, Rachel?

RACHEL (*calling*): Priscilla, is that you? Here I am, working in my rose garden!

PRISCILLA (*calling*): Come over a minute. I want to show you something!

RACHEL (*calling*): All right. (*She joins* PRISCILLA.) What is it, Priscilla?

PRISCILLA (*indicating*): Look! All ten of them. Aren't they something?

RACHEL (*happy for her friend*): I thought you had only nine?

PRISCILLA: The coin dealer called me today. The complete set!

RACHEL: I am so glad for you.

PRISCILLA (*happily*): For a time, it looked as if that tenth one never would show up.

> (The two friends freeze in a pose, admiring the coins.

DAVID *stands and looks over toward* REBECCA, *who lives down the street.*)

DAVID (*calling out*): Rebecca–a–a! Rebecca–a–a!

REBECCA (*calling out*): Whatcha want?

DAVID (*calling*): Whatcha doing?

REBECCA (*calling*): Nothing.

DAVID (*calling*): Wanta play catch?

REBECCA (*calling*): Okay!

(*They are both standing as if actually nearer each other. Speak normally.*)

REBECCA: For a while. Then I gotta go.

DAVID (*tossing ball. This tossing continues*): Catch. Where you going?

REBECCA (*disgusted*): To the *beauty* parlor.

DAVID (*also disgusted*): *Beauty* parlor? What for, for Pete's sake?

REBECCA: Not me. Mother. She won't leave me here by myself.

DAVID: Come over to my house! We'll climb the big tree. I found a bird's nest.

REBECCA: Really?

DAVID: Sure! Ask your mom.

REBECCA (*Calling. Wait for imaginary answers*): Mom, can I stay at David's? While you go to the beauty parlor, I mean. Thanks, Mom. (*To David*) I *can!*

(*She runs over to join DAVID. Both freeze.*)

PRISCILLA: Listen to those kids! Rachel, I think they ran through your rose garden.

RACHEL (*hurrying back to her place, calling out*): David! Rebecca! Don't run through my roses! Now, you know better than that.

REBECCA (*calling*): Yes, ma'am!

DAVID (*calling*): My ball fell out of the tree.

RACHEL (*calling*): Ball? What was a ball doing in a tree? Oh, never mind! But you stay out of those roses, you hear me?

> (*She freezes.*)

DAVID (*calling*): Yes, ma'am! (*In normal voice to* REBECCA) Always griping.

REBECCA: We didn't hurt her old rose! Did we?

> (*They freeze again.* PRISCILLA *joins* RUTH *and* JAMES.)

PRISCILLA: I just had to come over and thank you!

JAMES: For what?

PRISCILLA: That new dealer you told me about? He found the *tenth coin!*

RUTH: The set's complete? Oh, I know you are happy. Did you tell Rachel?

PRISCILLA: Right away. I'm so happy, I've told everyone in the neighborhood!

> (*They all freeze.*)

REBECCA: My mother ought to be home by now.

DAVID: Wanta go see?

REBECCA: Yeah. Maybe she'll let us have a popsicle!

> (*They run to* REBECCA's *place. Freeze.*)

RACHEL (*calling out, angrily*): I see you in my rose garden! All right! I'll just tell your mothers, that's what! (*Freeze.*)

DAVID: Old screechy Rachel!

REBECCA (*looking around*): The car's not here. Mom's not back.

DAVID: We better go back to my house, huh?

REBECCA: Yeah. Let's go *around* this time!

DAVID: Yeah. That old Rachel.

> (*They go to* DAVID's *place, this time passing between the spots for* RACHEL *and* PRISCILLA. *When they arrive,* DAVID *talks to an imaginary mother.*)

DAVID (*calling out*): Here I am, Mom! I was over at Rebecca's. Okay, we'll stay out front till you get back. (*Both freeze.*)

PRISCILLA: Well, I'd better get on home. Thanks again, neighbor!

JAMES: Any time.

RUTH: Come back.

PRISCILLA: 'Bye, now.

> (*She goes back to her place, smiling. Looks at her coins. Frantically counts them. Then again. One is missing. Looks on the floor under her stool, behind and on either side of it. Then she runs to* RACHEL.)

PRISCILLA (*frantically*): Rachel! Rachel!

RACHEL (*alarmed*): What is it, Priscilla?

PRISCILLA: My coins! One is missing!

RACHEL: *Missing?* Are you sure?

PRISCILLA: Sure I'm sure! One, two, three, four, five, six, seven, eight, nine, and that's all!

RACHEL: Did you look for it? *Good?*

PRISCILLA: Of course I looked good! Everywhere! What'll I do, Rachel? What'll I do?

RACHEL (*practically*): Don't lose your head, Priscilla. Don't panic. Here, sit down. (*She does.*) Now, *think.* I know they were all there when I left.

PRISCILLA: They were all there when I went over to Ruth and James's.

RACHEL: You went over to Ruth and James's?

PRISCILLA: Yes, to tell them the set was complete. They told me about that dealer. Remember?

RACHEL: Did you lock the door?

PRISCILLA (*thinking*): N–no. Just to go to Ruth and James's?

RACHEL: How long were you gone?

PRISCILLA: About twenty minutes. Possibly longer.

RACHEL: Then anybody could have gone in, Priscilla. *Anybody*!

PRISCILLA: Did you see anyone hanging around?

RACHEL: No. Not a soul except David and Rebecca—those kids.

(*They look at each other, shocked at their thoughts.*)

RACHEL: Oh, no! They wouldn't? You aren't thinking?

(PRISCILLA *waits a moment, then—*)

PRISCILLA (*calling out*): David! Rebecca!

DAVID (*calling*): Yes, ma'am?

PRISCILLA (*calling*): Please come here!

REBECCA: What's the matter with *her*?

(*All four crowd into Priscilla's spot.*)

PRISCILLA: David, Rebecca, do you see these coins?

REBECCA: Yes, ma'am.

PRISCILLA: There are *nine*. You can count them?

DAVID (*counts*): There are nine, all right.

PRISCILLA: A little while ago, there were *ten*. Does that mean anything special to you?

DAVID (*bewildered*): Ma'am?

RACHEL: I saw you running through my rose garden!

PRISCILLA: Did you go straight through, or did you come over here?

REBECCA (*shocked*): *No ma'am!*

PRISCILLA: Very well. You may go now.

> (*The children return to* DAVID'S. PRISCILLA *and* RACHEL *freeze.*)

REBECCA: David, she thinks we took her old coin!

DAVID (*unhappily*): What can we do?

REBECCA: I wish our moms were home. (*They freeze.*)

PRISCILLA: I hate to accuse those kids. Were they telling the truth? Oh, dear!

RACHEL: I didn't say it while they were here, but I *did* see them run through the yard between our houses.

PRISCILLA: You did? Oh, Rachel, I hate this. Maybe—maybe— (*calling out*) Ruth! James!

RUTH (*calling*): Yes, Priscilla?

PRISCILLA (*calling*): Did you see anyone around my house just a while ago?

JAMES (*calling*): When you were over here?

PRISCILLA (*calling*): Yes!

JAMES (*normal tone*): Did you see anyone, Ruth?

RUTH: Just those children. What are their names?

JAMES: I saw them, too. But no strangers.

RUTH: Neither did I.

JAMES (*calling*): Priscilla?

PRISCILLA (*calling*): Yes?

JAMES (*calling*): The only ones we saw in your yard were David and Rebecca, those kids in the block!

PRISCILLA (*calling*): Thanks! (*Normal tone*) Oh, Rachel, I don't know what to do.

RACHEL: I don't know what to advise you to do. They aren't *bad* kids. Well, I've got to go. Tell me later what you decide.

> (RACHEL *returns to her spot, freezes.* DAVID *and* RE-BECCA *come to* PRISCILLA.)

DAVID: Miss Priscilla—

PRISCILLA (*coldly*): Yes? What do you want?

DAVID (*miserably*): Miss Priscilla, Rebecca and me—

PRISCILLA: Well, go on!

REBECCA: You think we took your coin, but we didn't!

DAVID: No, ma'am! Rebecca and me—well, we did go through your yard—

REBECCA: But we didn't go in your house. We wouldn't go in your house!

PRISCILLA: Would you admit it if you did?

DAVID: If we did, why didn't we take *all* the coins?

PRISCILLA: You might think one would not be missed. But these are not ordinary coins.

REBECCA: But we *didn't*, Miss Priscilla!

PRISCILLA: Did you see anyone else around?

REBECCA: No, ma'am, nobody.

PRISCILLA (*coldly*): Well, then?

DAVID (*protesting*): If nobody came in and we didn't either, then the coin is still here!

PRISCILLA: No, it isn't. I looked. *Everywhere.*

DAVID: Not everywhere.

PRISCILLA (*firmly*): I looked everywhere!

DAVID: You didn't look where it *is.*

PRISCILLA: Young man, if—

DAVID (*interrupting*): Please show us where you looked.

PRISCILLA: Well—(*indicating under and behind and to each side of her stool*) Well, I looked here and here and here and here!

REBECCA (*pointing front*): Did you look there?

PRISCILLA: We weren't over there! Of course not.

DAVID: Then that's where it is. Why don't you look there?

(PRISCILLA *slowly walks in front of the stool. She looks about carefully, then pounces. Joyfully, she seems to put the coin back with the others on the seat.*)

PRISCILLA: It's here! It's found! Look! All my coins again!

(*The children look at each other, shrug, wave at each other, then each returns to his place, freezes. Meanwhile* PRISCILLA *has not stopped talking.*)

PRISCILLA (*continuing*): How could I have missed it? How could it have gotten out there? Aren't they lovely? Just look! Children—oh, they've gone. (*Calling out*) Rachel, come see! Ruth, James! Come look!

(*All gather around her stool, except the children.*)

RACHEL: You have your coin back! Oh, Priscilla!

JAMES: Who had it?

PRISCILLA (*embarrassed*): No one. It was here all the time.

RUTH: Where?

PRISCILLA (*pointing*): Over there. All the time.

RACHEL: I'm so glad those children didn't take it.

PRISCILLA (*protesting, trying to deny to herself her former attitude*): Of *course* not! Those are *nice* children!

RUTH (*bewildered*): I thought you said once they were nuisances?

JAMES: Hush, Ruth.

PRISCILLA: Anyway, I have my coins again, all lovely ten of them.

JAMES: Ruth and I are glad for you, Priscilla. We must go. Good night Priscilla.

RACHEL: Me, too. 'Night, Priscilla.

PRISCILLA: Good night, everyone.

> (*They all return to first positions and freeze. In six seconds they all leave the stage.*)

Questions for Talking

1. Do you like to share your pleasures with friends?

2. Do you want to tell somebody immediately when anything out of the ordinary happens?

3. Did you ever do something innocent that looked guilty? Did you feel guilty even though you knew you weren't?

4. Do you think David and Rebecca felt hurt at the unjust suspicion?

5. Is it hard to talk to grown-ups?

6. This ended happily for the woman. Do things always end happily?

7. Was anybody unhappy?

8. What does this little play say to you?

10

A Tree Is for Climbing

If you haven't read the Foreword for helpful suggestions, do so now. Playing time is 21 to 24 minutes. Scripture basis is Luke 19:1–10. Also see Luke 3:13; Exodus 22:1; Numbers 5:6–7; Ezekiel 34:16. The play has some characters not found in the Bible story. Zacchaeus was rich. He surely had servants. He was a publican, a tax collector, hated for his dealings. Names were chosen for these characters. The director will note that a number of boys and girls may be used in the crowd scenes. Lines for the Crowd are numbered in the script. Thus the director may combine them for any size crowd, renumbering.

The play will profit from biblical costuming. Props needed are a chair, a four- or five-foot ladder with a branch tied on, a scroll for Zacchaeus, two small bags of "money."

As in another play in this book (If a Mustard Seed) the character of Jesus may be heard rather than seen. The play is designed so that the one saying Jesus' lines will be concealed behind the Crowd. If the director wants the character seen, simply stage the scene in reverse, with "Jesus" (and some "followers" in that case) walking across stage in front of the Crowd. Zacchaeus then would be upstage behind everyone.

CAST: ZACCHAEUS, *a rich publican, an unusually small man;* HODESH, *his housekeeper-servant;* KETURAH, *his young maidservant;* ELAM, *a grain merchant;* ELHANAN, *a donkey trader;* VOICE OF JESUS; *the* CROWD.

> (*As the play begins,* ZACCHAEUS *is seated center, reading a scroll.*)

ZACCHAEUS (*calling*): Hodesh! Hodesh!

HODESH (*breathlessly entering left*): Yes, Master?

ZACCHAEUS (*irritably*): Isn't my dinner ready yet?

HODESH: Forgive us, Master. The bread is not yet done. That oven—

ZACCHAEUS: That oven again? With all the money I pay out, why can't I have an oven that bakes properly?

HODESH (*anxiously*): The workman said it is the drafts. He believes he has it fixed. But the bread is late. Also Keturah has not returned.

ZACCHAEUS: Where is Keturah? Why isn't she here where she belongs?

HODESH: Rachel from next door said there were fresh grapes at the stall by the Jerusalem gate. I sent Keturah—

ZACCHAEUS (*crossly*): Very well. But hurry. I'm hungry.

(HODESH *exits left.* ZACCHAEUS *begins reading. Suddenly we hear voices off left.*)

HODESH (*excited, off*): He *did*?

KETURAH: That's what they said!

HODESH: I *know* Bartimaeus!

KETURAH: Imagine! After all these years.

HODESH: Oh, how his father must rejoice.

ZACCHAEUS (*irritated by the loud chatter*): Hodesh! Hodesh!

KETURAH (*off, not hearing*): If only I'd been a little sooner—

HODESH: Then you'd have seen it happen. O Keturah!

ZACCHAEUS (*now angry*): Hodesh! Keturah! Will somebody answer me?

HODESH (*running in, followed by Keturah*): You called, Master?

ZACCHAEUS (*sarcastically and loudly*): What is going on out there?

HODESH (*excited*): Master, blind Bartimaeus can *see*!

KETURAH: The prophet from Nazareth, Master!

ZACCHAEUS What are you talking about, girl?

HODESH: Tell him Keturah.

KETURAH (*suddenly nervous and shy*): I – I – I–

ZACCHAEUS (*sarcastically*): Today, please.

KETURAH: Bar–Bartimaeus can see, Master.

HODESH: Bartimaeus, the blind beggar who sits outside the Jerusalem gate. That man from Nazareth—Jesus—restored his sight!

ZACCHAEUS: Nonsense. Some sort of trick. No one makes a blind man see. Kitchen talk. Where's my dinner?

HODESH (*subdued*): Immediately, Master. (*She goes off left. KETURAH is following, when there is a pounding right.*)

ZACCHAEUS: Keturah! The door! Before whoever it is breaks it down.

KETURAH (*hurrying right*): Yes, my lord.

(KETURAH *goes off right and is pushed back and aside by the entrance of an angry* ELAM, *a grain merchant.*)

ELAM: There you are, you—you thief!

ZACCHAEUS (*calmly*): Elam.

ELAM (*shouting in Zacchaeus' face*): What's going on down at that warehouse?

ZACCHAEUS (*innocently*): What warehouse?

ELAM: The warehouse where you've got my grain, that's what warehouse!

ZACCHAEUS: Your grain is safe. Don't worry.

ELAM: Don't *worry*? When *you've* got it? I want it. I want it now!

ZACCHAEUS: Naturally.

ELAM: Your men refused to give it to me! Something about not enough tax money.

ZACCHAEUS: Then what's the trouble?

ELAM (*pulling out a small bag of money*): Here's the tax set by the Romans for the amount of grain I imported. Now you send word to release that grain to me! How can I get it to my customers if it is held in your warehouse. Tell me that?

ZACCHAEUS (*sarcastically*): That *is* a problem, isn't it? But I can't turn that grain loose on an innocent public. It might be *bad*. Every sack has to be inspected.

ELAM: Zacchaeus, you know that is the best grain, fresh from Egypt!

ZACCHAEUS (*pretending concern*): You can't always tell with imported grain.

ELAM: When can I have it then?

ZACCHAEUS: Well, my men are busy. It may take a month.

ELAM (*shouting*): A *month*? In *that* warehouse? It can turn bad in a month.

ZACCHAEUS: Then I would be right to hold it. Besides, you know how careless some of my slaves are. They might spill it.

ELAM: Zacchaeus, you are the worst publican I deal with. That's saying a lot, too.

ZACCHAEUS: Thank you.

ELAM: Someday you'll get yours! How much will it cost me to get my grain out?

ZACCHAEUS: Twice the tax.

ELAM: *Twice* the tax?

ZACCHAEUS: One for me, one for Rome.

ELAM (*shouting and dancing around the calm Zacchaeus*): Crook! Thief! Vilest of publicans! Here's your blood money!

> (*He pulls out a second pouch and throws it at ZAC-CHAEUS who catches it and tucks it away.*)

Now release my grain!

ZACCHAEUS: Thank you, Elam. May you prosper. (*Calls*) Keturah!

> (*She runs in from the left.*)

KETURAH: Yes, Master?

ZACCHAEUS: Who is on the door tonight?

KETURAH: Jorah and Abi.

ZACCHAEUS: Run tell Jorah to go to the warehouse by the camel market. He's to tell the men there Elam is coming after his grain. They will release it.

ELAM (*sarcastically*): Without an inspection, Zacchaeus?

ZACCHAEUS (*innocently*): Everyone knows you are honest, Elam. Farewell.

> (*ELAM rushes off right. KETURAH tries to keep up. In a moment she returns.*)

KETURAH: Master, Jorah has gone. Elhanan, the donkey trader, is outside. He demands to see you at once.

ZACCHAEUS: Is my dinner ready?

KETURAH (*apologetically*): Not yet, Master.

ZACCHAEUS: Then show him in. Might as well get it over. But hurry that dinner.

KETURAH: Yes, Master. (*She goes right, returns with ELHANAN, then exits left.*)

ELHANAN (*bowing low*): Greetings, Zacchaeus.

ZACCHAEUS: I can spare but a moment.

ELHANAN: Then I will get right to my business. I want to bring in a herd of prime donkeys. They are not far—over in Bethany in Perea. The market is good now, and these are first-class animals.

ZACCHAEUS: So?

ELHANAN (*bluntly*): What's it going to cost me? I know the Roman tax, Zacchaeus. But what will your cut cost me?

ZACCHAEUS: Since you put it so delicately—these are prime beasts?

ELHANAN: The best.

ZACCHAEUS: Very well. Sell ten for me.

ELHANAN: *What!*

ZACCHAEUS: That's my price, take it or leave it.

ELHANAN (*angrily*): You robber! To bring in ten for you, besides the cost, there goes wages for extra men, extra food—

ZACCHAEUS: And the Roman tax on them. Too bad. That's it.

ELHANAN: I can't make a profit that way.

ZACCHAEUS: Then don't. Retire on your savings.

ELHANAN: What savings? All right! It's a deal.

ZACCHAEUS: That's a good fellow. I'll call my servant. Go in good health.

ELHANAN (*angrily*): I'll show myself out! Bloodsucker. You you care a lot for my health! (*He rushes off right.*)

ZACCHAEUS: Hodesh! Where is my supper?

(*Off left, talking is heard.*)

HODESH (*off, excited*): He *is*? Oh, thank you, Rachel.

KETURAH (*off*): Let's hurry! Will the Master let us go see?

ZACCHAEUS: Hodesh! Come here. (*She enters, followed by the excited* KETURAH.) What's going on?

HODESH: Rachel from next door—

ZACCHAEUS: Doesn't that woman ever stay home?

HODESH: Rachel says Jesus is coming through Jericho before he goes to Jerusalem.

ZACCHAEUS: That's hardly news to make me miss a meal.

KETURAH (*protesting*): But, Master, he's the one who gave Bartimaeus his sight!

HODESH: They say he healed ten lepers in Galilee, and in Judea he raised a man from the dead.

ZACCHAEUS: Tales, tales.

HODESH: No, Master, they even say the man was named Lazarus, and Rachel says her master knows the family in Bethany. That is the one in Galilee.

ZACCHAEUS: Rachel again!

KETURAH: He has followers, Master, and one of them is a publican like you.

ZACCHAEUS (*interested*): A publican? So.

HODESH: They even say he praised publicans over Pharisees once! At least that's what Rachel heard.

ZACCHAEUS: I wonder what we did for news before Rachel? So he likes publicans, does he?

HODESH (*hesitating*): Not—exactly.

ZACCHAEUS (*unheeding*): Then he can't be all bad. I may look at him myself when he goes through. Since Rachel next door is our news source, tell her to alert us.

KETURAH: Yes, Master. When he—he comes, may we, Hodesh and I, go see him, too?

ZACCHAEUS (genially): I don't know why not. It isn't often we have such excitement in Jericho. Now, what about my dinner?

HODESH: Ready, Master.

> (ZACCHAEUS exits left followed by HODESH and KETURAH, who takes the chair off with her. The lights go off just long enough for someone to place the ladder at right front, then the lights come on again. The CROWD enters from the right in small excited groups. They move about talking to each other until Jesus is seen coming.)

CROWD 1: Have you ever seen the Nazarene?

CROWD 2: Once. Several months ago. At a distance.

CROWD 3: Are you sure he's coming? Down this street, I mean?

CROWD 4: That's what I heard. It is all I know.

CROWD 5: What does he look like?

CROWD 6: They say he's not so handsome.

CROWD 7: Oh, I heard different. I heard he's tall, has piercing eyes, and strong hands.

CROWD 8: Where did you hear that. The way I heard it, he's middling height and a soft talker. Who knows who's in the right?

CROWD 9: I've seen Peter, one of his followers. What a temper!

CROWD 10: Is that the big one? From Galilee?

CROWD 11: Yes, near Capernaum. Great fishing there.

CROWD 12: What was that about the Nazarene healing lepers?

CROWD 13: They say the scribes and lawyers are always after him.

CROWD 14: So are the Pharisees. I'd hate to have them after me.

CROWD 15: Never heard of him doing any harm. Nothing bad.

(ELAM *and* ELHANAN *enter right and join the crowd.*)

ELAM: Too bad he can't use his magic on some black hearts I know!

ELHANAN: A knife between that publican's ribs would do us more good.

(ZACCHAEUS, HODESH, KETURAH *enter left. People step aside as they come across, looking away and muttering.*)

ELAM: Here's your chance. Who would see you in this crowd?

ELHANAN: Don't be a fool! We'd be the first suspected.

ELAM: Us and a hundred more.

CROWD 16: That's Zacchaeus, the publican.

CROWD 17: That little squirt? I thought he'd be ten feet tall with eight-inch fangs.

ELAM (*overhearing*): He may as well be. Ten denarii to anyone who roughs him up!

CROWD 18: Ten denarii?

ELHANAN: Watch out, Elam! You're asking for trouble.

CROWD 19 (*shoving against* ZACCHAEUS): Out of my way.

KETURAH (*trying to come between* CROWD 19 *and* ZACCHAEUS): Master, Master, go inside, quickly! Hodesh!

(HODESH *joins her, and they stand protecting* ZACCHAEUS.)

HODESH: Get back, you—you ruffians! This is my master Zacchaeus!

CROWD 20: We know. The publican cheat, that's who he is!

CROWD 21: Robber!

CROWD 22: Thief!

CROWD 23: Extortioner!

> (*crowding the three menacingly and joined by others*)

CROWD 24: Hang him! Hang the lover of Rome!

HODESH (*shouting*): Soldiers! Guards!

CROWD 25: You're wasting your breath, woman! We can string him up before they get here and be long gone!

HODESH (*shouting*): Soldiers! Guards! This way!

KETURAH: Master, run for it! Run!

CROWD 26 (*looking right*): He's coming. I see him! Look, Jesus is coming!

> (*Instantly the CROWD runs right, then slowly spreads across the stage, their backs to the audience as they look right, down the "street." All begin talking to each other, ad lib, about his looks, miracles, etc. Let them create lines. Make it sound like a busy hum. ZACCHAEUS is on the audience side, his servants with him. Then the girls go to see down the street, leaving him alone. He jumps up and down, trying to see or trying to push in but no one will let him.*)

ZACCHAEUS: I can't see. I can't see. Let me in!

> (*When nothing helps, he sees ladder, exclaims "A tree!" and climbs up, looks right. We know when Jesus has reached the area for the crowd falls silent.*)

VOICE OF JESUS: Who is that? Look up in that tree! Who is he?

CROWD 27: That's Zacchaeus, the publican, may his soul rot!

VOICE: Oh? (*calls*) Zacchaeus? Zacchaeus!

ZACCHAEUS (*suprised*): Y–yes?

VOICE: Zacchaeus, this *is* you up in that tree?

ZACCHAEUS: Y–yes!

VOICE: Why are you up there?

ZACCHAEUS: To see you, O Nazarene. I couldn't see over—them.

VOICE: Why wouldn't they let you through?

> (CROWD *creates lines telling all they have against* ZAC-
> CHAEUS, *all talking at once.*)

VOICE (*calmly*): Quiet, friends! Zacchaeus?

ZACCHAEUS: I–I hear you, Lord.

VOICE: Zacchaeus, look down. Do you see me? Do you truly
see me?

ZACCHAEUS (*looking down to Jesus*): Yes, Lord. I see your eyes,
Lord. Oh, yes.

VOICE: Zacchaeus, come down here where I am.

ZACCHAEUS: They won't let me through, Lord.

VOICE: Yes, they will. Come on down. Zacchaeus, I am going
home with you. My disciples and I will dine with you, if
this is agreeable.

ZACCHAEUS (*happily*): Yes, Lord. Yes, indeed!

VOICE: Come show us the way. I am waiting.

> (ZACCHAEUS *climbs down. Reluctantly the* CROWD *lets
> him through. He goes off left, with his servants, and
> apparently the followers of Jesus. When they have gone,
> the* CROWD *breaks up into groups, facing the audience.*)

CROWD 28: Did you see that?

CROWD 29: Maybe the Nazarene didn't know—

CROWD 30: Of course he knew! He's done this sort of thing
before.

CROWD 31: If he's going to associate with publicans and sinners,
I don't want anything to do with him!

CROWD 32: Me either.

CROWD 33: Aw, let's give him a chance. Those people he cured—

CROWD 34: Not me! He must be a quack! Let's go!

> (*The* CROWD *moves off right, murmuring until they are off. The lights go off, the ladder is removed, and the chair put back, all in seconds. The lights come up.* ZACCHAEUS *is in the chair. There is a pounding right.* KETURAH *runs across from left and brings in* ELAM. *He strides over and throws a small money pouch into* ZACCHAEUS' *lap.*)

ELAM: All right! What is this? Why did you send me this money?

ZACCHAEUS: It is very simple. I cheated you, Elam.

ELAM: You cheat me every time we do business. What's so different this time?

ZACCHAEUS: The Nazarene made me see. This money is fourfold restitution—according to the law.

ELAM (*suspiciously*): I don't believe you. One meal with him, and you are a changed man? Ha!

ZACCHAEUS: Then you don't know him.

ELAM: You're up to something.

ZACCHAEUS: My dear Elam, never again will I cheat you. Believe me.

ELAM (*angrily*): What are you trying to pull?

ZACCHAEUS: Trust me. Wait and see.

ELAM: From now on I'll be watching you every minute! And don't you forget it.

> (*He rushes off right, passing* ELHANAN *on his way in.*)

Out of my way!

ELHANAN: What's wrong with him? Oh, well, it doesn't matter. I've come to pay up.

ZACCHAEUS: Pay only the Roman tax.

ELHANAN (*alarmed*): You aren't going to take my whole herd?

ZACCHAEUS: Only the Roman tax. Keep the rest for yourself. I don't want to cheat you.

ELHANAN (*suspiciously*): You're up to something new. I'd better catch up with Elam. See what he thinks.

(*He exits right quickly.* KETURAH *and* HODESH *enter.*)

HODESH: I heard, Master. What's the matter with those two?

ZACCHAEUS: Just human, Hodesh.

KETURAH: Why can't they see you've changed?

ZACCHAEUS: Can you, Keturah?

KETURAH (*shyly*): Yes, Master. This is a kinder house.

ZACCHAEUS: Thank you, Keturah. I may be in the only place people will see I am different.

HODESH: It isn't fair.

ZACCHAEUS: But it is human. When you do wrong, you have to prove yourself to others. I'll be patient—for a lifetime if necessary.

KETURAH: Because of—the Nazarene?

ZACCHAEUS: Because of the Nazarene.

Questions for Talking

1. Zacchaeus worked for his country's conquerers. Could this happen today?

2. If you had lived then, would you have liked Zacchaeus?

3. Why didn't people believe he had changed?

4. If a boy or girl who is called "bad" changes, do others believe him?

5. Were Elam and Elhanan free from fault? Is anyone all good or all bad?